THE FUNERAL

THE FUNERAL
A SERVICE OF WITNESS
TO THE RESURRECTION

The Worship of God

Supplemental Liturgical Resource 4

Prepared by

The Office of Worship
for the
Presbyterian Church (U.S.A.)
and the
Cumberland Presbyterian Church

Published by
The Westminster Press
Philadelphia

Unless otherwise indicated in the Sources, scripture quotations are from the Revised Standard Version of the Bible, copyrighted 1946, 1952, © 1971, 1973 by the Division of Christian Education of the National Council of the Churches of Christ in the U.S.A., and are used by permission.

For Acknowledgments, see pages 103–104.

Published by The Westminster Press®
Philadelphia, Pennsylvania

PRINTED IN THE UNITED STATES OF AMERICA

4 6 8 9 7 5 3

Library of Congress Cataloging-in-Publication Data

Presbyterian Church (U.S.A.)
 The funeral.

 (Supplemental liturgical resource ; 4)
 Bibliography: p.
 1. Funeral service—Presbyterian Church.
2. Presbyterian Church (U.S.A.)—Liturgy—Texts.
3. Cumberland Presbyterian Church—Liturgy—Texts.
4. Presbyterian Church—Liturgy—Texts. 5. Death—
Religious aspects—Christianity—Bibliography.
I. Office of Worship for the Presbyterian Church
(U.S.A.) and the Cumberland Presbyterian Church.
II. Cumberland Presbyterian Church. III. Title.
IV. Series: Presbyterian Church (U.S.A.).
Supplemental liturgical resource ; 4.
BX8969.5.P74   1986a   264'.05137   86-1536
ISBN 0-664-24034-8 (pbk.)

CONTENTS

PREFACE

In 1980, the antecedent denominations of the Presbyterian Church (U.S.A.) took action to begin the process to develop "a new book of services for corporate worship, including a Psalter, hymns, and other worship aids." The churches asked that over the "next several years a variety of worship resources be made available . . . for trial use throughout the church before any publication is finalized." In this action the church expressed a hope that such a book and the process leading to it "would provide a new instrument for the renewal of the church at its life-giving center." Subsequent action by the Cumberland Presbyterian Church made it a partner in the project.

The Funeral: A Service of Witness to the Resurrection is the fourth volume in the series of trial-use liturgical resources that is resulting from the General Assembly actions. Previous volumes include: *The Service for the Lord's Day* (Supplemental Liturgical Resource 1), *Holy Baptism and Services for the Renewal of Baptism* (Supplemental Liturgical Resource 2), and *Christian Marriage* (Supplemental Liturgical Resource 3). Other resources being developed include daily prayer, the psalms, the Christian year, ordination, ministry to the sick and dying, the lectionary, and service music. When the series of resources is completed, the material that will have appeared will be further revised and combined in a new book of services.

In developing the resources, guidance on worship policy is given by the Advisory Council on Discipleship and Worship through its Committee on Worship.

A task force of persons with expertise in the particular subject of the resource to be developed is appointed by the Administrative Committee of the Office of Worship to prepare a manuscript on an assigned portion of the church's liturgy. In the fall of 1982, a task force was appointed to prepare the funeral liturgy. *The Funeral: A Service of Witness to the Resurrection* is the result of the work of that task force.

Those who served on the task force that prepared *The Funeral: A Service of Witness to the Resurrection* were Lewis A. Briner, chairperson; J. Michael Krech; James Hastings Nichols; Jesse G. Truvillion; Jeannette Wessler; LindaJo McKim, consultant; and Harold M. Daniels, staff.

Each manuscript that is developed in the Supplemental Liturgical Resource series is carefully reviewed by the Worship Committee of the Advisory Council on Discipleship and Worship, which makes suggestions for its revision. Members of the Worship Committee reviewing *The Funeral: A Service of Witness to the Resurrection* were J. Barrie Shepherd, chairperson; Moffett Swaim Churn; Jay Dee Conrad; Melva W. Costen; Frances M. Gray; Robert S. Moorhead; Irene Overton; Franklin E. Perkins; Donald W. Stake; Helen Wright; James G. Kirk, staff; Elizabeth J. Villegas, staff; and Harold M. Daniels, adjunct staff.

The Funeral: A Service of Witness to the Resurrection was extensively field-tested. Suggestions were also sought from liturgical scholars both in the Reformed and in other traditions. The evaluations and suggestions that were received contributed greatly to the improvement of this resource, and we are therefore indebted to many people for their invaluable assistance.

Responding to the field-testing and review, the task force prepared the final draft of this resource and presented it to the Administrative Committee of the Office of Worship. The Administrative Committee, which has overseen the work of the task force during the years the resource was being developed, then approved the manuscript for publication. Those who served on the Administrative Committee during the time *The Funeral: A Service of Witness to the Resurrection* was being developed were Melva W. Costen; Lucile L. Hair (former chairperson); Helen Hamilton, Collier S. Harvey; James G. Kirk; Wynn McGregor; Ray Meester; Robert D. Miller; David C. Partington (current chairperson); Dorothea Snyder (former chairperson); Robert Stigall; Darius L. Swann; James Vande Berg; Harold M. Daniels, staff; and Marion L. Liebert, staff.

We invite your evaluation of this resource presented to the church for trial use as it anticipates a new book of services. Send your comments to the Office of Worship, 1044 Alta Vista Road, Louisville, Kentucky 40205.

HAROLD M. DANIELS, Director
Office of Worship

MINISTRY AT THE TIME OF DEATH

When death is near, the minister should be notified so that the ministry of the church may be extended.

The service for the Renewal of Baptism for the Sick and the Dying (Holy Baptism and Services for the Renewal of Baptism, *pp. 92–93) may be used instead of this service. Or, portions of it may be included in this service following the Lord's Prayer.*

The minister greets those present saying:

The grace of our Lord Jesus Christ
and the love of God
And the fellowship of the Holy Spirit
be with you.   *2 Cor. 13:14*

And also with you.

This or a similar prayer is said.

Gracious God, look on _____ ,
whom you claimed as your own through Baptism.
Comfort *him/her* with the promise of life eternal,
made sure in the death and resurrection of your Son,
Jesus Christ our Lord.

Amen.

The Lord's Prayer is said.

One of the following is said.

Lord Jesus Christ,
deliver your servant _____ from all evil,
and set *him/her* free from every bond;
that *he/she* may rest with all your saints
in the joy of your eternal home
for ever and ever.

Amen.

Gracious God,
you are nearer than hands or feet,
closer than breathing.
Sustain with your presence our *brother/sister* _____ .
Help *him/her* now to trust your goodness
and claim your promise of life everlasting.
Cleanse *him/her* of all sin
and remove all burdens.
Grant *him/her* the sure joy of your salvation,
through Jesus Christ our Lord.

Amen.

Almighty God,
by your power Jesus Christ was raised from death.
Watch over our *brother/sister* _____ .
Fill *his/her* eyes with your light
to see, beyond human sight, a home within your love
where pain is gone
and frail flesh turns to glory.
Banish fear.
Brush tears away.
Let death be gentle as nightfall,
promising a day when songs of joy
shall make us glad to be together with Jesus Christ
who lives in triumph,
the Lord of life eternal.

Amen.

_____ , our *brother/sister* in the faith,
we entrust you to God who created you.
May you return to the one who formed us out of the dust of the earth.
Surrounded by the angels and triumphant saints,
may Christ come to meet you
as you go forth from this life.

Christ, the Lord of glory,
who was crucified for you,
bring you freedom and peace.

Christ, the High Priest,
who has forgiven all your sins,
keep you among his people.

Christ, the Son of God,
who died for you,
show you the glories of his eternal kingdom.

Christ, the Good Shepherd,
enfold you with his tender care.
May you see your redeemer face to face
and enjoy the sight of God for ever.

Amen.

For use when a life-support system is withdrawn:

God of compassion and love,
you have breathed into us the breath of life
and have given us the exercise of our minds and wills.
In our frailty we surrender all life to you from whom it came,
trusting in your gracious promises;
through Jesus Christ our Lord.

Amen.

The minister lays his or her hand on the head of the dying person:

Depart in peace, O *brother/sister*;
In the name of God the Father who created you;
In the name of Christ who redeemed you;
In the name of the Holy Spirit who sanctifies you.

May you rest in peace,
and dwell forever with the Lord.

And

Into your hands, O merciful Savior,
we commend your servant _____ .
Acknowledge, we humbly beseech you,
a sheep of your own fold,
a lamb of your own flock,
a sinner of your own redeeming.
Receive *him/her* into the arms of your mercy,
into the blessed rest of everlasting peace,
and into the glorious company of the saints in light.

Amen.

The following prayer is said:

O Lord, support us all the day long
of this troubled life,
until the shadows lengthen
and the evening comes
and the busy world is hushed,
and the fever of life is over,
and our work is done.
Then, in your mercy,
grant us a safe lodging,
and a holy rest,
and peace at the last;
through Jesus Christ our Lord.

Amen.

Prayers may be said for the family and friends of the dying, such as one of the following. Those present may be invited to offer prayers.

Almighty God, our creator and redeemer,
you are our comfort and strength.
You have given us our *brother/sister* _____
to know and to love in our pilgrimage on earth.

Uphold us now as we entrust *him/her*
to your boundless love and eternal care.
Assure us that not even death
can separate us from your infinite mercy.
Deal graciously with us who mourn,
that we may truly know your sure consolation
and learn to live in confident hope of the resurrection;
through your Son, Jesus Christ our Lord.

Amen.

Lord God,
look kindly upon us in our sorrow
for this life being taken from us,
and gather our pain into your peace.
Heal our memories,
be present to our grieving,
and overcome all our doubts.
Awaken our gratitude for your gifts of love and tenderness.
As we are able to receive them,
teach us the lessons of life that can be learned in death.
We pray through Christ our Lord.

Amen.

Lord Jesus,
we wait for you to grant us your comfort and peace.
We confess that we are slow to accept death
as an inevitable part of life.
We confess our reluctance
to surrender this friend and loved one to your eternal care.
You, Lord Jesus, know the depth of our sorrow;
you also wept for a dead friend.
Let the Holy Spirit, the Comforter you promise,
come upon us now.
Grant us your love and peace as we reach out to console one another.
Be our companion as we live through the painful days ahead;
and even as we mourn,
may all we feel, think, say, and do bear witness to our faith.

Amen.

Lead, kindly Light,
our only hope in darkness.
Heal the wounds of sorrow
and renew our trust in your goodness.
Enable us to be grateful
for the ties that bind us to the one we are now losing.
Renew our strength each day
to seek your will
and lean upon your mercy.
Keep us ever in the communion of saints
and in the promise of life eternal,
through Christ our Lord.

Amen.

Prayers with parents after the birth of a stillborn child or the death of a newly born child.

Merciful God,
you strengthen us by your power and wisdom.
Be gracious to _____ and _____ in their grief,
and surround them with your unfailing love;
that they may not be overwhelmed by their loss,
but have confidence in your goodness,
and courage to meet the days to come;
through Jesus Christ our Lord.

Amen.

Gracious God,
in darkness and in light,
in trouble and in joy,
help us to trust your love,
to serve your purpose,
and to look forward in hope to your heavenly kingdom;
through Jesus Christ our Lord.

Amen.

A blessing, such as the following, is given.

The Lord bless you and keep you.
The Lord be kind and gracious to you.
The Lord look upon you with favor
and give you peace.   *Num. 6:24–26*

Amen.

COMFORTING THE BEREAVED

It is appropriate for family and friends to gather for prayers, in the home or funeral establishment, on the day or night before the funeral. This order may be used for such occasions. Psalms and lessons suggested in the funeral rite may be included. Prayers in the funeral rite, comparable to those in this service, may be substituted. The service may be led by the minister or another representative of the church.

Scripture sentences, such as the following, are said:

May the God of hope
fill you with all joy and peace in believing,
so that you may abound in hope
by the power of the Holy Spirit.   *Rom. 15:13*

God is our refuge and strength,
a very present help in trouble.   *Ps. 46:1*

The eternal God is your dwelling place,
and underneath are the everlasting arms.   *Deut. 33:27*

Blessed are those who mourn,
for they shall be comforted.   *Matt. 5:4*

Praise be to the God and Father of our Lord Jesus Christ,
the Father of mercies and God of all comfort,
who comforts us in all our sorrows,
so that we can comfort others in their sorrow,
with the consolation we have received from God.   *2 Cor. 1:3–4*

A prayer, such as the following, is said:

Eternal God,
our help in every time of trouble,
send your Holy Spirit to comfort and strengthen us,
that we may have hope of life eternal
and trust in your goodness and mercy,
through Jesus Christ our Lord.

Amen.

Or

Jesus said, "Come to me, all who labor
and are heavily burdened,
and I will give you rest."   *Matt. 11:28*

Let us pray for our *brother/sister* _____ ,
that *he/she* may rest from *his/her* labors,
and enter into the light of God's eternal rest.

Receive, O Lord, your servant,
for *he/she* returns to you.
May *he/she* hear your words of welcome,
"Come, you blessed of my Father,"
and receive the unfading crown of glory.
May the angels surround *him/her*
and the saints welcome *him/her* in peace.

**Into your hands, O Lord,
we commend our *brother/sister*_____ .**

Gracious God,
in whose presence live all who die in the Lord,
receive our *brother/sister* _____ ,
into your merciful arms,
and the joys of your heavenly home.
May *he/she* and all the departed rest in your peace.

Amen.

> *A hymn may be sung.*
>
> *A psalm may be read, or sung.*

One or more lessons from Scripture may be read. An interpretation of the lessons, and reflections on the life of the deceased, may follow. Informal conversation with the family may be appropriate.

One or more of the following prayers may be said.

Holy God,
Lord of life and death,
you made us in your image
and hold us in your care.
We thank you for your servant _____ ,
for the gift of *his/her* life,
and for the love and mercy *he/she* received from you and gave to us.
Especially we praise you for your love in Jesus Christ,
who died and rose from the grave,
to free us from evil,
and give us life eternal.
Grant that when our time on earth is ended,
we may be united with all the saints
in the joys of your eternal home,
through Jesus Christ our Lord.

Amen.

Almighty God, source of all mercy and giver of comfort,
deal graciously with those who mourn,
that, casting all their sorrow on you,
they may know the consolation of your love;
through your Son, Jesus Christ our Lord.

Amen.

Creator God,
your Holy Spirit prays for us
even when we do not know how to pray.
Send your Spirit to comfort us in our need and loss,
and help us to commend_____ to your merciful care;
through Jesus Christ our Lord.

Amen.

At the death of a child:

Loving God,
your beloved Son took children into his arms and blessed them.
Give us grace, we pray,
that we may entrust _____ to your never-failing care and love,
and bring us all to your heavenly kingdom;
through Jesus Christ our Lord.

Amen.

The Lord's Prayer is said.

The leader says this blessing:

The Lord bless us,
defend us from all evil,
and bring us to everlasting life.

Amen.

OUTLINE OF THE FUNERAL:
A SERVICE OF WITNESS TO THE RESURRECTION

Placing of the Pall
Sentences of Scripture
Psalm, Hymn, or Spiritual
Prayer
  Confession and Pardon
Scripture Readings
  Prayer for Illumination
  Old Testament Lesson
  Psalm
  Epistle Lesson
  Gospel Lesson
Sermon
Creed
Hymn
Prayers

——————— *Or* ———————▼

Lord's Prayer

Preparation of the Table (during
  psalm, hymn, or spiritual)
Great Prayer of Thanksgiving,
  followed by the Lord's Prayer
Breaking of the Bread
Communion of the People

◄————————————————————┘

Commendation
Blessing
Procession (Psalm, Hymn, or Biblical Song)

THE FUNERAL:
A SERVICE OF WITNESS TO THE RESURRECTION

When death occurs, the pastor of the congregation should be informed as soon as possible, in order to provide appropriate consolation and support to the family and friends, and to assist in all the arrangements for the funeral.

Except for compelling reasons, the service for a believing Christian is normally held in the church, at a time when the congregation can be present. When the deceased was not known to be a believer or had no connection with a church, then it is appropriate to hold the service elsewhere and to omit or adapt portions as seems fitting. (The ceremonies and rites of social or fraternal organizations, if any, should occur at some other time and place.)

Family members, friends, or members of the congregation may be invited by the minister to share in the service.

This order is intended for use with the body or ashes of the deceased present, but it may be adapted for use as a memorial service. The committal may follow or precede this service, as preferred. When a coffin is present, it should be closed before the service, and covered with a pall.

PLACING OF THE PALL

As the pall is placed over the coffin by the pallbearers, the following is said or intoned:

For as many of you as were baptized into Christ
have put on Christ. *Gal. 3:27*

In *his/her* baptism _____ put on Christ;
in the day of Christ's coming,
he/she shall be clothed with glory.

Or

When we were baptized in Christ Jesus,
we were baptized into his death.
We were buried therefore with him by baptism into death,
so that as Christ was raised from the dead by the glory of the Father,

we too might live a new life.
For if we have been united with Christ in a death like his,
we shall certainly be united with him in a resurrection like his.

Rom. 6:3–5

Appropriate music may be offered as the people gather.

If there is a PROCESSION into the place of worship, the minister leads it as the congregation sings a psalm or a hymn. Or the minister may say or intone sentences of Scripture while leading the procession.

If the coffin or urn of ashes has already been brought in, the minister begins the service with one or more of the following or similar sentences.

SENTENCES OF SCRIPTURE

Our help is in the name of the Lord,
who made heaven and earth. Ps. 124:8

Praise the Lord.
The Lord's name be praised.

When we were baptized in Christ Jesus,
we were baptized into his death.
We were buried therefore with him by baptism into death,
so that as Christ was raised from the dead by the glory of the Father,
we too might live a new life.
For if we have been united with him in a death like his,
we shall certainly be united with him in a resurrection like his.

Rom. 6:3–5

I am the resurrection and the life, says the Lord.
Those who believe in me shall live,
even though they die,
and whoever lives and believes in me shall never die. John 11:25–26

I am the Alpha and the Omega,
the beginning and the end,
the first and the last.
I died and behold I am alive for evermore;
and I have the keys of Death and Hades.
Because I live, you will live also. Rev. 21:6; 22:13;
1:17–18; John 14:19

Come to me, all who labor and are heavily burdened,
and I will give you rest.   *Matt. 11:28*

Praise be to the God and Father of our Lord Jesus Christ,
whose great mercy gave us new birth into a living hope
by the resurrection of Jesus Christ from the dead!
The inheritance to which we are born
is one that nothing can destroy or spoil or wither.   *1 Peter 1:3–4*

God is our refuge and strength,
a very present help in trouble.
Therefore we will not fear.   *Ps. 46:1*

Peace I leave with you;
my peace I give to you;
not as the world gives do I give to you.
Let not your hearts be troubled,
neither let them be afraid.   *John 14:27*

As a father pities his children,
so the Lord pities those who fear him.   *Ps. 103:13*
As a mother comforts her child,
so I will comfort you.   *Isa. 66:13*

The eternal God is your dwelling place,
and underneath are the everlasting arms.   *Deut. 33:27*

I am sure that neither death, nor life,
nor angels, nor principalities,
nor things present, nor things to come,
nor powers, nor height, nor depth,
nor anything else in all creation,
will be able to separate us from the love of God
in Christ Jesus our Lord.   *Rom. 8:38–39*

Fear not,
I am the first and the last,
and the living one;
I died, and behold I am alive for evermore.   *Rev. 1:17–18*

Fear not, for I am with you,
be not dismayed, for I am your God;
I will strengthen you, I will help you,
I will uphold you with my victorious right hand.   *Isa. 41:10*

Blessed are those who mourn,
for they shall be comforted.   *Matt. 5:4*

Praise be to the God and Father of our Lord Jesus Christ,
the Father of mercies and God of all comfort,
who comforts us in all our sorrows,
so that we can comfort others in their sorrow,
with the consolation we have received from God.   *2 Cor. 1:3–4*

We believe that Jesus died and rose again;
and so it will be for those who have died in Christ.
God will raise them to be with the Lord for ever.
Comfort one another with these words.   *1 Thess. 4:14, 17–18*

If we live, we live unto the Lord;
and if we die, we die unto the Lord.
Whether we live therefore, or die,
we are the Lord's.   *Rom. 14:7–8*

Blessed are the dead who die in the Lord, says the Spirit.
They rest from their labors,
and their works follow them.   *Rev. 14:13*

PSALM, HYMN, OR SPIRITUAL

The congregation may sing a psalm, hymn of praise, or spiritual.

PRAYER

One or more of the following prayers may be said.

The Lord be with you.

And also with you.

Let us pray.

Eternal God, Father of our spirits,
in whose presence there is no darkness and no death:
We worship and adore you, the everliving God.

Lord Jesus Christ,
the resurrection and the life,
who tasted death for every one
and who brought life and immortality to light,
we praise your name for victory over death and the grave.

Holy Spirit,
author and giver of life,
Comforter of those who sorrow,
in you is our sure confidence
and our everlasting hope.

Before you we worship and adore, saying,
blessing and glory and wisdom
and thanksgiving and honor
and power and strength
be to our God for ever and ever.

Amen.

O God, who gave us birth,
you are ever more ready to hear than we are to pray.
You know our needs before we ask,
and our ignorance in asking.
Show us now your grace,
that as we face the mystery of death
we may see the light of eternity.

Speak to us once more your solemn message of life and of death.
Help us to live as those who are prepared to die.
And when our days here are ended,
enable us to die as those who go forth to live,
so that living or dying,
our life may be in Jesus Christ our risen Lord.

Amen.

Eternal God, we bless you for the great company
of all those who have kept the faith,
finished their race,
and who now rest from their labor.
We praise you for those dear to us
whom we name in our hearts before you. . . .
Especially we thank you for _____ ,
whom you have now received into your presence.

Help us to believe where we have not seen,
trusting you to lead us through our years.
Bring us at last with all your saints
into the joy of your home,
through Jesus Christ our Lord.

Amen.

Eternal God,
amid all the changes of life you alone remain the same.
We acknowledge the uncertainty of our life on earth.
We are given a mere handful of days,
and our span of life seems nothing in your sight.
All flesh is as grass;
and all its beauty is like the flower of the field.
The grass withers, the flower fades;
but the word of our God will stand forever.
Our hope is in you, O God.
Even in the valley of the shadow of death, you are with us.
O Lord, let us know our end
and the number of our days,
that we may know how fleeting life is.
Hear our prayer,
and turn your ear to our cry.
Be not deaf to our tears,
for we live as strangers before you,
wandering pilgrims as all our ancestors were.
But you are the same
and your years shall have no end.

Amen.

And/or a PRAYER OF CONFESSION may be said:

Let us now ask God to cleanse our hearts,
to redeem our memories,
and to renew our confidence in the goodness of God.

**Holy God, you see us as we are,
and know our inmost thoughts.
We confess that we are unworthy of your gracious care.
We forget that all life comes from you**

and that to you all life returns.
We have not always sought or done your will.

We have not lived as your grateful children,
nor loved as Christ loved us.
Apart from you, we are nothing.
Only your grace can sustain us.

Lord, in your mercy, forgive us,
heal us and make us whole.
Set us free from our sin,
and restore to us the joy of your salvation
now and forever. Amen.

The people may pray silently.

Assurance of God's forgiving grace is declared by the minister:

Who is in a position to condemn?
Only Christ,
and Christ died for us,
Christ rose for us,
Christ reigns in power for us,
Christ prays for us.   *Rom. 8:34*

Anyone in Christ becomes a new person altogether;
the past is finished and gone,
everything has become fresh and new.   *2 Cor. 5:17*

Amen.

Or

The mercy of the Lord
is from everlasting to everlasting.
I declare to you, in the name of Jesus Christ,
you (*we*) are forgiven.

May the God of mercy,
who forgives you (*us*) all your (*our*) sins,
strengthen you (*us*) in all goodness,
and by the power of the Holy Spirit
keep you (*us*) in eternal life.

Amen.

The people may sing a thankful response to the mercy of God.

SCRIPTURE READINGS

Before the reading of the Scripture lessons, a PRAYER FOR ILLUMI-NATION may be said by the reader:

Source of all true wisdom,
calm the troubled waters of our hearts,
and still all other voices but your own,
that we may hear and obey
what you tell us in your Word,
through the power of your Spirit.
Amen.

Or

Eternal God,
your love for us is everlasting;
you alone can turn the shadow of death
into the brightness of the morning light.
Help us to turn to you with reverent and believing hearts.
In the stillness of this hour, speak to us of eternal things,
so that, hearing the promises in Scripture,
we may have hope
and be lifted above our darkness and distress
into the light and peace of your presence;
through Jesus Christ our Lord.
Amen.

> *Appropriate Scripture is read from the OLD TESTAMENT. (See pp. 57–58, 61–64.)*
>
> *After the reading from the Old Testament lesson, a PSALM may be sung or said. (See pp. 58, 64–69.)*
>
> *Appropriate Scripture is read from the NEW TESTAMENT concluding with a reading from the GOSPELS. (See pp. 59–60, 69–74.)*

SERMON

A brief sermon may be preached, proclaiming the gospel, followed as desired by expressions of gratitude to God for the life of the deceased.

CREED

The congregation stands and says or sings the Apostles' Creed or an affirmation of faith:

I believe in God, the Father almighty,
    creator of heaven and earth.

I believe in Jesus Christ, his only Son, our Lord.
    He was conceived by the power of the Holy Spirit
        and born of the Virgin Mary.
    He suffered under Pontius Pilate,
        was crucified, died, and was buried.
    He descended to the dead.
    On the third day he rose again.
    He ascended into heaven,
        and is seated at the right hand of the Father.
    He will come again to judge the living and the dead.

I believe in the Holy Spirit,
    the holy catholic church,
    the communion of saints,
    the forgiveness of sins,
    the resurrection of the body,
    and the life everlasting. Amen.

HYMN

A hymn of confident faith may be sung by the congregation.

PRAYERS

Prayers of thanksgiving, supplication, and intercession like the following are offered. Additional prayers may be found on pp. 54–56.

O God of grace,
you have given us new and living hope in Jesus Christ.

We thank you that by dying
Christ destroyed the power of death,
and by rising from the grave
opened the way to eternal life.

Help us to know that because he lives,
we shall live also;
and that neither death nor life,
nor things present nor things to come
shall be able to separate us from your love
in Christ Jesus our Lord.

Amen.

O God,
before whom generations rise and pass away,
we praise you for all your servants
who, having lived this life in faith,
now live eternally with you.

Especially we thank you for your servant _____ ,
for the gift of *his/her* life,
for all in *him/her* that was good and kind and faithful,
for the grace you gave *him/her*,
that kindled in *him/her* the love of your dear name,
and enabled *him/her* to serve you faithfully.
[*Here mention may be made of characteristics or service.*]

We thank you that for *him/her* death is past and pain ended,
and that *he/she* has now entered the joy you have prepared;
through Jesus Christ our Lord.

Amen.

Almighty God,
in Jesus Christ you promised many rooms within your house.
Give us faith to see beyond touch and sight
some sure sign of your kingdom,
and, where vision fails,
to trust your love which never fails.
Lift our heavy sorrow
and give us good hope in Jesus,
so we may bravely walk our earthly way,

and look forward to glad reunion in the life to come,
through Jesus Christ our Lord.

Amen.

Or

For our *brother/sister* _____ ,
let us pray to our Lord Jesus Christ
who said, "I am the resurrection and the life."

Lord, you consoled Martha and Mary in their distress;
draw near to us who mourn for _____ ,
and dry the tears of those who weep.

Hear us, Lord.

You wept at the grave of Lazarus, your friend;
comfort us in our sorrow.

Hear us, Lord.

You raised the dead to life;
give to our *brother/sister* eternal life.

Hear us, Lord.

You promised paradise to the repentant thief;
bring _____ to the joys of heaven.

Hear us, Lord.

Our *brother/sister* was washed in baptism
and anointed with the Holy Spirit;
give *him/her* fellowship with all your saints.

Hear us, Lord.

He/she was nourished at your table on earth,
welcome *him/her* at your table in the heavenly kingdom.

Hear us, Lord.

Comfort us in our sorrows at the death of _____ ;
let our faith be our consolation,
and eternal life our hope.

Amen.

At the death of a child:

Loving Father,
you are nearest to us when we need you most.
In this hour of sorrow we turn to you,
knowing that you love us,
and trusting your perfect wisdom.

We bless you for the gift of this child
for *his/her* baptism into your church,
for the joy *he/she* gave all who knew *him/her*
for the precious memories that will abide with us,
and for the assurance that *he/she* lives forever
in the joy and peace of your presence.

Amen.

*If the Lord's Supper is not to follow, the prayers end with the LORD'S
PRAYER, and the service continues with the commendation.*

When the service includes the Lord's Supper, it continues on p. 37.

COMMENDATION

The minister says:

You only are immortal,
the creator and maker of all.
We are mortal,
formed of the earth, and to earth shall we return.
This you ordained when you created us, saying,
"You are dust,
and to dust you shall return."
All of us go down to the dust;
yet even at the grave we make our song:
Alleluia, alleluia, alleluia.

Give rest, O Christ, to your servant with all your saints,
where there is neither pain nor sorrow nor sighing,
but life everlasting.

Facing the body, the minister shall say:

Holy God,
by your creative power
you gave us the gift of life,
and in your redeeming love
you have given us new life in Christ.
We commend _____
to your merciful keeping
in the faith of Christ our Lord
who died and rose again to save us,
and who now lives and reigns with you
and the Holy Spirit in glory forever.

Amen.

Or

Into your hands, O merciful Savior,
we commend your servant _____ .
Acknowledge, we humbly pray,
a sheep of your own fold,
a lamb of your own flock,
a sinner of your own redeeming.
Receive *him/her* into the arms of your mercy,
into the blessed rest of everlasting peace,
and into the glorious company of the saints in light.

Amen.

BLESSING

Let the minister say this blessing:

Go in peace,
and may the God of peace—
who brought again from the dead our Lord Jesus,
the great shepherd of the sheep,
by the blood of the eternal covenant—
equip you with everything good,
that you may do God's will,
working in you what is pleasing in God's sight,
through Jesus Christ to whom be glory for ever and ever.

Heb. 13:20–21

Amen.

Or

The peace of God, which passes all understanding,
keep your hearts and minds
in the knowledge and love of God,
and of God's Son Jesus Christ our Lord.   *Phil. 4:7*

May the blessing of God almighty,
the Father, Son, and Holy Spirit,
remain with you always.

Amen.

Or

May God in endless mercy
bring the whole church,
the living and departed,
to a joyful resurrection
in the fulfillment of the eternal kingdom.

Amen.

> *The procession forms and leaves the church, the minister preceding
> the coffin. As the procession leaves the church, a psalm, a hymn, or
> this biblical song may be sung or said.*

**Lord, now you let your servant go in peace;
your word has been fulfilled:
my own eyes have seen the salvation
which you have prepared in the sight of every people:
a light to reveal you to the nations
and the glory of your people Israel.**   *Luke 2:29–32*

**Glory to the Father, and to the Son,
and to the Holy Spirit,
as it was in the beginning,
is now, and will be forever. Amen.**

When the Lord's Supper is included, the service continues from page 34 as follows:

A psalm, hymn, or spiritual may be sung as the table is prepared. The bread and wine may be brought to the table or uncovered if already in place.

GREAT PRAYER OF THANKSGIVING

Standing at the table, the minister says or sings:

The Lord be with you.

And also with you.

Lift up your hearts.

We lift them to the Lord.

Let us give thanks to the Lord our God.

It is right to give our thanks and praise.

It is truly right and our greatest joy
to give you thanks and praise,
O holy Father, creator and ruler of the universe.
You are the source of all life,
creating all things in your wisdom,
and sustaining them by your power.
You made us in your image,
forming us from the dust of the earth,
and breathing into us the breath of life.

You made us to know you,
to love and to serve you;
but we rebelled against you,
seeking to be our own god.
In your mercy, you did not forsake us.
You made a covenant with us,
claiming us as your people,
and promising faithfulness as our God.
Through the prophets you called us to return to your ways.
Out of your great love for the world,
you gave your only Son to redeem us,
and to open the way to eternal life.

He formed for himself a new people
born of water and the Spirit.
In ways beyond number you have shown us your mercy.

Therefore, we praise you,
joining our voices with choirs of angels,
and with all the faithful of every time and place,
who forever sing to the glory of your name:

Holy, holy, holy Lord, God of power and might,
heaven and earth are full of your glory.
  Hosanna in the highest.

Blessed is he who comes in the name of the Lord.
  Hosanna in the highest.

Blessed are you, O Lord our God,
for sending your Son Jesus Christ.
He lived as one of us,
knew our joy, our pain and sorrow,
and died our death.
By his death on the cross
you revealed that your love has no limit.
By raising him from the grave
you conquered death, the last enemy,
crushed all evil powers,
and gave new life to the world.
By his victory
you comfort us with the hope of eternal life,
and assure us that neither death nor life,
nor things present nor things to come,
can separate us from your love in Christ Jesus our Lord.

Risen and ascended, Christ is alive forevermore,
and by the power of the Holy Spirit is with us always.
Reigning with you in glory,
Christ intercedes for us,
our high priest and our advocate.

> *The words of institution may be said here or in relation to the breaking*
> *of the bread.*

[We give you thanks that on the night before he died,
Jesus took bread.

After giving thanks to you, he broke it,
and gave it to his disciples, saying,
"Take, eat.
This is my body, given for you.
Do this in remembrance of me."

In the same way he took the cup, saying,
"This cup is the new covenant sealed in my blood,
shed for you for the forgiveness of sins.
Do this in remembrance of me."]

In remembrance of your mighty acts in Jesus Christ,
we take from your creation this bread and this wine
and celebrate his death and resurrection,
as we await the day of his coming.
Accept this our sacrifice of praise and thanksgiving,
as a living and holy offering of ourselves,
dedicated to your service,
that our lives may proclaim the mystery of faith.

**Dying you destroyed our death,
rising you restored our life.
Lord Jesus, come in glory.**

Gracious God,
pour out your Holy Spirit upon us,
and upon these your gifts of bread and wine,
that the bread we break
and the cup we bless
may be the communion of the body and blood of Christ.
By your Spirit make us one with Christ,
and one with all who share this feast,
until we feast together in the joy of his eternal kingdom.

Remember our *brother/sister* _____ ,
whose baptism is now complete in death.
Bring *him/her,* and all who have died in the peace of Christ,
into your eternal joy and light.

Strengthen us to run with determination
the race that lies before us,
our eyes fixed on Jesus,
on whom our faith depends from beginning to end,

so that, when this mortal life is ended,
we may, with the faithful from every time and place,
receive the unfading crown of glory,
through your Son Jesus Christ.

Through Christ, with Christ, in Christ,
in the unity of the Holy Spirit,
all glory and honor, praise and adoration are yours,
Father almighty, God of all ages,
now and forever.

Amen.

The Lord's Prayer is said.

Our Father in heaven,
  hallowed be your name,
  your kingdom come,
  your will be done,
    on earth as in heaven.
Give us today our daily bread.
Forgive us our sins
  as we forgive those
    who sin against us.
Save us from the time of trial
  and deliver us from evil.
For the kingdom, the power,
  and the glory are yours,
  now and forever. Amen.

Our Father, who art in heaven,
  hallowed be thy name,
  thy kingdom come,
  thy will be done,
    on earth as it is in heaven.
Give us this day our daily bread;
and forgive us our debts,
  as we forgive our debtors;
and lead us not into temptation,
  but deliver us from evil.
For thine is the kingdom,
  and the power, and the glory,
    forever. Amen.

BREAKING OF THE BREAD

If the words of institution were included in the great prayer of thanksgiving, the minister holds the bread in full view of the people, saying:

Because there is one loaf,
we, many as we are, are one body;
for it is one loaf of which we all partake.

The minister breaks the bread in full view of the congregation.

When we break the bread,
is it not a sharing in the body of Christ?

The minister lifts the cup.

When we give thanks over the cup,
is it not a sharing in the blood of Christ?
(1 Cor. 10:16–17)

If the words of institution were not included in the great prayer of thanksgiving, the minister breaks the bread in the presence of the people, saying:

The Lord Jesus, on the night of his arrest, took bread,
and after giving thanks to God,
he broke it and said,
"This is my body, given for you.
Do this in remembrance of me."

The minister lifts the cup, saying:

In the same way, he took the cup after supper, saying,
"This cup is the new covenant sealed in my blood.
Whenever you drink it,
do it in remembrance of me."

Every time you eat this bread and drink this cup,
you proclaim the death of the Lord,
until he comes.
(1 Cor. 11:23–26; Luke 22:19–20)

Holding out both the bread and the cup to the people, the minister says:

The gifts of God
for the people of God.

COMMUNION OF THE PEOPLE

As the people are served the bread and wine, the following words may be said:

The bread of heaven.

Amen.

The cup of salvation.

Amen.

During the serving of the sacrament, the Agnus Dei ("Jesus, Lamb of God"), which follows, or psalms, hymns, or spirituals may be sung, or silence kept.

Jesus, Lamb of God:
  have mercy on us.
Jesus, bearer of our sins:
  have mercy on us.
Jesus, redeemer of the world:
  give us your peace.

Lamb of God, you take away the sins of the world: have mercy on us.
Lamb of God, you take away the sins of the world: have mercy on us.
Lamb of God, you take away the sins of the world: grant us peace.

After all are served, the following prayer may be said:

Almighty God,
we thank you that in your great love
you have fed us with the spiritual food and drink
of the body and blood of your Son Jesus Christ,
and have given us a foretaste of the heavenly banquet.
Grant that this Sacrament may be to us
a comfort in affliction,
and a pledge of our inheritance
in that kingdom where there is no death,
neither sorrow nor crying,
but the fullness of joy with all your saints;
through Jesus Christ our Savior.

Amen.

The service resumes with the commendation on p. 34.

OUTLINE OF
COMMITTAL SERVICE

Sentences
Committal
Prayers
Blessing

COMMITTAL SERVICE

If preferred, the committal service may take place before the general service. In either case, the minister precedes the body (or ashes) to the appointed place, saying one or more of the following sentences:

SENTENCES

The Sun of Righteousness is gloriously risen,
giving light to those who sat in darkness
and in the shadow of death.   *Based on Luke 1:78–79*

The Lord will guide our feet into the way of peace,
having taken away the sin of the world.   *Based on Luke 1:79*

I know that my Redeemer lives,
and that at the last he will stand upon the earth.   *Job 19:25*

Fear not,
I am the first and the last,
and the living one;
I died, and behold I am alive for evermore.   *Rev. 1:17–18*
Because I live, you will live also.   *John 14:19*

If we live, we live unto the Lord;
and if we die, we die unto the Lord.
Whether we live therefore, or die,
we are the Lord's.   *Rom. 14:7–8*

Christ has promised:
All whom the Father gives to me will come to me;
no one will ever be turned away who believes in me.   *John 6:37*

My heart, therefore, is glad,
and my spirit rejoices;
my body also shall rest in hope.   *Ps. 16:9*

You will show me the path of life;
in your presence there is fullness of joy,
and in your right hand are pleasures for evermore.   *Ps. 16:11*

Christ is risen from the dead,
trampling down death by death,
and giving life to those in the grave.

> *When there is no other service than the committal service, a prayer
> (such as those on pp. 26–29) may be said here after the people have
> gathered.*

COMMITTAL

Earth burial

*The coffin is lowered into the grave or placed in its resting place.
While earth is cast upon the coffin, the minister says:*

In sure and certain hope of the resurrection to eternal life,
through our Lord Jesus Christ,
we commend to almighty God our *brother/sister* _____ ,
and we commit *his/her* body to the ground:
earth to earth, ashes to ashes, dust to dust.

Blessed are the dead who die in the Lord, says the Spirit.
They rest from their labors,
and their works follow them.   *Rev. 14:13*

Burial at sea

As the body is lowered into the water, the minister says:

In sure and certain hope of the resurrection to eternal life,
through our Lord Jesus Christ,
we commend to almighty God our *brother/sister* _____ ,
and we commit *his/her* body to the deep:

Blessed are the dead who die in the Lord, says the Spirit.
They rest from their labors,
and their works follow them.   *Rev. 14:13*

At a cremation service

As the body is placed in the crematory, the minister says:

In sure and certain hope of the resurrection to eternal life,
through our Lord Jesus Christ,
we commend to almighty God our *brother/sister* _____ ,
and we commit *his/her* body to be dissolved:
ashes to ashes, dust to dust.

Blessed are the dead who die in the Lord, says the Spirit.
They rest from their labors,
and their works follow them.   *Rev. 14:13*

At a columbarium

As the ashes are placed in their resting place, the minister says:

In sure and certain hope of the resurrection to eternal life,
through our Lord Jesus Christ,
we commend to almighty God our *brother/sister* _____ ,
and we commit *his/her* ashes to their final resting place.

Blessed are the dead who die in the Lord, says the Spirit.
They rest from their labors,
and their works follow them.   *Rev. 14:13*

The Lord's Prayer may be said.

Our Father in heaven,
  hallowed be your name,
  your kingdom come,
  your will be done,
    on earth as in heaven.
Give us today our daily bread.
Forgive us our sins
  as we forgive those
    who sin against us.
Save us from the time of trial
  and deliver us from evil.
For the kingdom, the power,
  and the glory are yours,
  now and forever. Amen.

Our Father, who art in heaven,
  hallowed be thy name,
  thy kingdom come,
  thy will be done,
    on earth as it is in heaven.
Give us this day our daily bread;
and forgive us our debts,
  as we forgive our debtors;
and lead us not into temptation,
  but deliver us from evil.
For thine is the kingdom,
  and the power, and the glory,
  forever. Amen.

PRAYERS

The minister says one or more of the following or other appropriate prayers:

O Lord, support us all the day long
of this troubled life,
until the shadows lengthen
and the evening comes
and the busy world is hushed,
and the fever of life is over,
and our work is done.
Then, in your mercy,
grant us a safe lodging,
and a holy rest,
and peace at the last;
through Jesus Christ our Lord.

Amen.

O God,
you have designed this world,
and know all things good for us.
Give us such faith

that, by day and by night,
in all times and in all places,
we may without fear
entrust those who are dear to us
to your never-failing love,
in this life and in the life to come;
through Jesus Christ our Lord.

Amen.

God of all mercies
and giver of all comfort,
look graciously, we pray, on those who mourn,
that, casting all their care on you,
they may know the consolation of your love;
through Jesus Christ our Lord.

Amen.

Gracious Father,
in darkness and in light,
in trouble and in joy,
help us to trust your love,
to serve your purpose,
and to look forward in hope to your heavenly kingdom;
through Jesus Christ our Lord.

Amen.

Almighty God,
Father of the whole family in heaven and on earth,
stand by those who sorrow;
that, as they lean on your strength,
they may be upheld,
and believe the good news of life beyond life;
through Jesus Christ our Lord.

Amen.

God of boundless compassion,
our only sure comfort in distress,
look tenderly upon your children
overwhelmed by loss and sorrow.

Lighten our darkness with your presence
and assure us of your love.
Enable us to see beyond this place and time
to your eternal kingdom,
promised to all who love you in Christ the Lord.

Amen.

Merciful God,
you heal the broken in heart
and bind up the wounds of the afflicted.
Strengthen us in our weakness,
calm our troubled spirits,
and dispel our doubts and fears.
In Christ's rising from the dead
you conquered death and opened the gates to everlasting life.
Renew our trust in you
that by the power of your love
we shall one day be brought together again
with our *brother/sister.*
Grant this we pray through Jesus Christ our Lord.

Amen.

God of all consolation,
our refuge and strength in sorrow,
by dying, our Lord Jesus Christ conquered death;
by rising from the grave he restored us to life.
Enable us to go forward in faith to meet him,
that, when our life on earth is ended,
we may be united with all who love him
in your heavenly kingdom,
where every tear will be wiped away;
through Jesus Christ our Lord.

Amen.

O God,
whose mercies are beyond number,
let your Holy Spirit lead us
with the company of the whole church
in holiness and righteousness,

in confidence of a living faith,
and in the strength of a sure hope.
Most gracious Lord,
may we live in favor with you,
and in perfect love with all;
through Jesus Christ our Lord.

Amen.

God, whose days are without end,
help us always to remember how brief life is
and that the hour of our death is known only to you.
Lead us, by your Holy Spirit,
to live in holiness and justice all our days.
Then, after serving you in the fellowship of your church,
in faith, hope, and love,
may we enter with joy into the fullness of your kingdom,
through Jesus Christ our Lord.

Amen.

Rest eternal grant *him/her*, O Lord;
and let light perpetual shine upon *him/her*.

Amen.

> *At the committal of a child:*

Loving God,
your beloved Son took children into his arms and blessed them.
Give us grace, we pray,
that we may entrust _____ to your never-failing care and love,
and bring us all to your heavenly kingdom;
through Jesus Christ our Lord.

Amen.

> *At the committal of a child:*

Loving God,
give us faith to believe,
though this child has died,
that you welcome *him/her*

and will care for *him/her*,
until, by your mercy,
we are together again in the joy of your promised kingdom;
through Jesus Christ our Lord.

Amen.

BLESSING

The minister dismisses the people with one of the following blessings.

The grace of the Lord Jesus Christ,
and the love of God,
and the fellowship of the Holy Spirit
be with you all.   *2 Cor. 13:14*

Amen.

    Or

The Lord bless you and keep you.
The Lord be kind and gracious to you.
The Lord look upon you with favor
and give you peace.   *Num 6:24–26*

Amen.

    Or

The peace of God, which passes all understanding,
keep your hearts and minds
in the knowledge and love of God,
and of God's Son Jesus Christ our Lord.   *Phil. 4:7*

May the blessing of God almighty,
the Father, Son, and Holy Spirit,
remain with you always.

Amen.

Or

Go in peace,
and may the God of peace—
who brought again from the dead our Lord Jesus,
the great shepherd of the sheep,
by the blood of the eternal covenant—
equip you with everything good,
that you may do God's will,
working in you what is pleasing in God's sight,
through Jesus Christ to whom be glory for ever and ever.

Heb. 13:20–21

Amen.

ALTERNATE LITURGICAL TEXTS

This section provides liturgical texts that may be substituted for portions of the funeral rite.

AFFIRMATION OF FAITH

One of the following may be substituted for the creed (p. 31).

A.

The Te Deum ("You are God . . ."), which follows, may be sung by the congregation as an affirmation of faith following the sermon, or before or after the creed (p. 31).

You are God: we praise you;
You are the Lord: we acclaim you;
You are the eternal Father:
All creation worships you.
To you all angels, all the powers of heaven,
Cherubim and Seraphim, sing in endless praise:
  Holy, holy, holy Lord, God of power and might,
  heaven and earth are full of your glory.
The glorious company of apostles praise you.
The noble fellowship of prophets praise you.
The white-robed army of martyrs praise you.
Throughout the world the holy Church acclaims you;

Father, of majesty unbounded,
your true and only Son, worthy of all worship,
and the Holy Spirit, advocate and guide.

You, Christ, are the king of glory,
the eternal Son of the Father.
When you became human to set us free
you did not spurn the Virgin's womb.
You overcame the sting of death,
and opened the kingdom of heaven to all believers.
You are seated at God's right hand in glory.
We believe that you will come, and be our judge.
Come then, Lord, and help your people,
bought with the price of your own blood,
and bring us with your saints
to glory everlasting.

B.

Leader:

Who shall separate us from the love of Christ?
Shall tribulation or distress?
or persecution or famine?
or nakedness or peril or sword?

People:

No, in all these things we are more than conquerors
through him who loved us.
For we are sure that neither death, nor life,
nor angels, nor principalities,
nor things present, nor things to come,
nor powers, nor height, nor depth,
nor anything else in all creation,
will be able to separate us from the love of God
in Christ Jesus our Lord. Amen   *Rom. 8:35, 37–39*

C.

We believe there is no condemnation
for those who are in Christ Jesus;
and we know that in everything God works for good
with those who love him,
who are called according to his purpose.
We are sure that neither death, nor life,

nor angels, nor principalities,
nor things present, nor things to come,
nor powers, nor height, nor depth,
nor anything else in all creation,
will be able to separate us
from the love of God
in Christ Jesus our Lord. Amen.   *Rom. 8:1, 28, 38–39*

D.
This is the good news which we have received,
in which we stand,
and by which we are saved,
if we hold it fast:
that Christ died for our sins according to the scriptures,
that he was buried,
that he was raised on the third day,
and that he appeared first to the women,
then to Peter, and to the Twelve,
and then to many faithful witnesses.

We believe that Jesus is the Christ,   *1 Cor. 15:1–6*
the Son of the living God.   *Mark 16:9 (16:1–9)*
Jesus Christ is the first and the last,   *Matt. 16:16*
the beginning and the end;   *Rev. 22:13*
he is our Lord and our God. Amen.   *John 20:28*

PRAYERS

*One of the following prayers may be substituted for any of the prayers
following the creed (pp. 31–34).*

A.
Almighty God,
you call your people together
into the household of faith.
Give to your whole church
in heaven and on earth
your light and your peace.

Hear us, Lord.

Grant that all
who have been baptized into Christ's death and resurrection
may die to sin and rise to newness of life,
and that through the grave and gate of death
we may pass with him to our joyful resurrection.

Hear us, Lord.

Grant to us who are still in our pilgrimage,
and who walk as yet by faith,
that your Holy Spirit may lead us
in holiness and righteousness all our days.

Hear us, Lord.

Grant to all who mourn
a sure confidence in your loving care,
that, casting all their sorrow on you,
they may know the consolation of your love.

Hear us, Lord.

Grant us grace
to entrust _____ to your never-failing love
which sustained *him/her* in this life.
Receive *him/her* into the arms of your mercy,
and remember *him/her*
according to the favor you bear for your people.

Amen.

Prayers for use at the funeral of an infant or child:

Holy God,
your goodness is everlasting,
and your mercies never fail.
Yours is the beauty of childhood
and yours is the fullness of years.
Comfort us in our sorrow,
strengthen us with hope,
and breathe peace into our troubled hearts.
Assure us that the love in which we rejoiced for a time is not lost,
and that this child is with you,
safe in your eternal love and care.

We ask this in the name of Jesus Christ,
who took little children into his arms and blessed them.

Amen.

O God,
we thank you for the love that cares for us in life
and watches over us in death.
May we in faith and hope
give back to you the life which in love was given to us.
We bless your name for our Savior's joy in little children
and for the assurance that of such is the kingdom of heaven.
We believe that in death, as in life,
they are in his holy keeping.

In our sorrow
make us strong to commit ourselves, and those we love,
to your never-failing care.
In our perplexity
may we trust where we cannot understand.
In our loneliness
may we remember this child with thanks and love,
trusting that you will keep that which we have committed unto you,
until the eternal morning breaks
through Jesus Christ our Lord.

Amen.

Blessed Jesus, lover of children,
in lowliness of heart we cry to you for help.
Expecting the life of a child,
we have witnessed *his/her* sudden death.
Our despair is profound
and we know you weep with us in our loss.
Help us to hear your consoling voice
as we listen to the truth of Scripture.
Give healing to our grief,
O merciful Savior.

Amen.

APPROPRIATE SCRIPTURE PASSAGES

*The following readings are particularly appropriate for use in the funeral service, and ministry with the dying and bereaved. An asterisk * indicates that the text of that particular reading is included in this resource (pp. 61–74).*

Old Testament

*Job 19:23–27	I know that my redeemer lives
Isa. 25:6–9	God will swallow up death forever
Isa. 26:1–4, 19	God will keep them in perfect peace
*Isa. 40:1–11, 28–31	Comfort my people
*Isa. 40:28–31	Those who wait for the Lord shall renew their strength
Isa. 43:1–3a, 18–19, 25	When you pass through the waters
Isa. 44:6–8	I am the first and the last
Isa. 55:1–3, 6–13	Ho, everyone who thirsts
Isa. 61:1–4, 10–11	The Spirit of the Lord is upon me
*Isa. 65:17–25	I create new heavens and a new earth
Lam. 3:19–26, 31–36	My affliction and roaming
Dan. 12:1–3	Many of those who sleep in the dust shall awake
Joel 2:12–13, 23–24, 26–29	Turn to me with all your heart

Some have found this passage from an Apocryphal book useful in certain circumstances:

Wisdom of Solomon 3:1–7, 9; 5:15–16	The souls of the righteous are in the hand of God

At the loss of a child:

Zech. 8:1–8	Children playing in the streets of the city
*Isa. 65:17–25	I create new heavens and a new earth

For those whose faith is unknown:

*Eccl. 3:1–15	For everything there is a season
Lam. 3:1–9, 19–26	The Lord's steadfast love

Psalms

Psalms appropriate for singing or reading in the service include the following:

Ps. 16:5–11	The Lord is my chosen portion
*Ps. 23	The Lord is my shepherd
Ps. 27:1, 4–9a, 13–14	The Lord is my light and my salvation
Ps. 39:4–5, 12	Lord, let me know my end
Ps. 42:1–6a	As a hart longs for flowing streams
Ps. 43	Give judgment for me, O God
*Ps. 46:1–5, 10–11	A very present help in trouble
*Ps. 90:1–10, 12	Teach us to number our days
Ps. 91	The one who dwells in the shelter of the Most High
*Ps. 103	Bless the Lord, O my soul
Ps. 106:1–5	O give thanks to the Lord
Ps. 116:1–9, 15	My delight is in the Lord
Ps. 118	Open the gates of righteousness
*Ps. 121	I lift up my eyes to the hills
*Ps. 130	Out of the depths I cry to the Lord
*Ps. 139:1–12	Whither shall I go from thy Spirit?
Ps. 145	I will exalt you, O God my King
Ps. 146	Hallelujah! praise the Lord, O my soul

Epistles

Rom. 5:1–11	Hope does not disappoint
Rom. 6:3–9	Baptized into Christ's death, raised to live with him
*Rom. 8:14–23, 31–39	Nothing can separate us
*Rom. 14:7–9, 10b–12	Whether we live or die, we are the Lord's
1 Cor. 15:3–8, 12–20a	Christ raised from the dead
1 Cor. 15:20–24	In Christ shall all be made alive
*1 Cor. 15:20–26, 35–38, 42–44, 50, 53–58	Death is swallowed in victory
1 Cor. 15:35–44	The natural body and the spiritual body
1 Cor. 15:50–57	We shall all be changed
*2 Cor. 4:16—5:1	Visible things are transitory, invisible things permanent
2 Cor. 5:1–10	From God we have a house not made with hands
Eph. 1:11—2:1, 4–10	Saved by grace through faith
Phil. 3:7–11	Knowing him and the power of his resurrection
Phil. 3:20–21	Our citizenship is in heaven
Col. 3:1–17	Set your mind on the things above
*1 Thess. 4:13–18	The comfort of Christ's coming
2 Tim. 2:8–13	If we died with him, we shall also live with him
Heb. 2:14–18	Christ was tempted in every way
Heb. 11:1–3, 13–16; 12:1–2	Faith, the pilgrimage, the cloud of witnesses
1 Peter 1:3–12	Without seeing Christ you love him
1 Peter 3:18–22; 4:6	Christ's ministry to the spirits in prison
1 John 3:1–3	We are children of God
Rev. 7:2–3, 9–17	These are they who have come out of the great tribulation
Rev. 14:1–3, 6–7, 12–13	Rest for the saints
*Rev. 21:1–4, 22–25; 22:3–5	A new heaven and a new earth
Rev. 22:1–5	The Lord God will be their light

For those whose faith is unknown:

Rom. 2:12–16	The law written on the heart
*Rom. 14:7–9, 10c–12	None of us live to ourselves

Gospels

Matt. 5:1–12a	The Beatitudes
Matt. 11:25–30	Hidden from the wise, revealed to babes
Matt. 25:1–13	Wise and foolish virgins
Matt. 25:31–46	The Last Judgment
Luke 7:11–17	Jesus raises the son of the widow of Nain
Luke 18:15–17	We enter the kingdom only as children
*Luke 23:33, 39–43	Today you will be with me in Paradise
John 3:16–21	God so loved the world
John 5:24–29	Whoever hears and believes has eternal life
John 6:37–40	Whoever comes to me I will by no means cast out
John 6:47–58	Whoever believes in me has eternal life
*John 11:17–27	I am the resurrection and the life
John 11:38–44	Lazarus raised from the dead
*John 14:1–6, 25–27	Let not your hearts be troubled

At the loss of a child:

*Matt. 18:1–5, 10	The greatest in the kingdom of heaven
*Mark 10:13–16	Let the children come to me

For those whose faith is unknown:

Matt. 25:31–46	As you did it to one of the least of these

SELECTED SCRIPTURE READINGS

All readings are from the Revised Standard Version of the Bible.

Old Testament

Oh that my words were written!
    Oh that they were inscribed in a book!
Oh that with an iron pen and lead
    they were graven in the rock for ever!
For I know that my Redeemer lives,
    and at last he will stand upon the earth;
    and after my skin has been thus destroyed,
    then from my flesh I shall see God,
    whom I shall see on my side,
        and my eyes shall behold, and not another.
    My heart faints within me!

Job 19:23–27

For everything there is a season, and a time for every
    matter under heaven:
a time to be born, and a time to die;
a time to plant, and a time to pluck up what is planted;
a time to kill, and a time to heal;
a time to break down, and a time to build up;
a time to weep, and a time to laugh;
a time to mourn, and a time to dance;

a time to cast away stones, and a time to gather stones
together;
a time to embrace, and a time to refrain from embracing;
a time to seek, and a time to lose;
a time to keep, and a time to cast away;
a time to rend, and a time to sew;
a time to keep silence, and a time to speak;
a time to love, and a time to hate;
a time for war, and a time for peace.
What gain has the worker from his toil?

I have seen the business that God has given to the sons of men to be busy with. He has made everything beautiful in its time; also he has put eternity into man's mind, yet so that he cannot find out what God has done from the beginning to the end. I know that there is nothing better for them than to be happy and enjoy themselves as long as they live; also that it is God's gift to man that every one should eat and drink and take pleasure in all his toil. I know that whatever God does endures for ever; nothing can be added to it, nor anything taken from it; God has made it so, in order that men should fear before him. That which is, already has been; that which is to be, already has been; and God seeks what has been driven away.

Ecclesiastes 3:1–15

Comfort, comfort my people, says your God.
Speak tenderly to Jerusalem,
    and cry to her
that her warfare is ended,
    that her iniquity is pardoned,
that she has received from the LORD's hand
    double for all her sins.

A voice cries:
"In the wilderness prepare the way of the LORD,
    make straight in the desert a highway for our God.
Every valley shall be lifted up,
    and every mountain and hill be made low;
the uneven ground shall become level,
    and the rough places a plain.
And the glory of the LORD shall be revealed,
    and all flesh shall see it together,
    for the mouth of the LORD has spoken."

A voice says, "Cry!"
  And I said, "What shall I cry?"
All flesh is grass,
  and all its beauty is like the flower of the field.
The grass withers, the flower fades,
  when the breath of the LORD blows upon it;
  surely the people is grass.
The grass withers, the flower fades;
  but the word of our God will stand for ever.

Get you up to a high mountain,
  O Zion, herald of good tidings;
lift up your voice with strength,
  O Jerusalem, herald of good tidings,
  lift it up, fear not;
say to the cities of Judah,
  "Behold your God!"
Behold, the Lord GOD comes with might,
  and his arm rules for him;
behold, his reward is with him,
  and his recompense before him.
He will feed his flock like a shepherd,
  he will gather the lambs in his arms,
he will carry them in his bosom,
  and gently lead those that are with young.

                                    Isaiah 40:1–11

Have you not known? Have you not heard?
The LORD is the everlasting God,
  the Creator of the ends of the earth.
He does not faint or grow weary,
  his understanding is unsearchable.
He gives power to the faint,
  and to him who has no might he increases strength.
Even youths shall faint and be weary,
  and young men shall fall exhausted;
but they who wait for the LORD shall renew their strength,
  they shall mount up with wings like eagles,
they shall run and not be weary,
  they shall walk and not faint.

                                  Isaiah 40:28–31

For behold, I create new heavens
and a new earth;
and the former things shall not be remembered
or come into mind.
But be glad and rejoice for ever
in that which I create;
for behold, I create Jerusalem a rejoicing,
and her people a joy.
I will rejoice in Jerusalem,
and be glad in my people;
no more shall be heard in it the sound of weeping
and the cry of distress.
No more shall there be in it
an infant that lives but a few days,
or an old man who does not fill out his days,
for the child shall die a hundred years old,
and the sinner a hundred years old shall be accursed.
They shall build houses and inhabit them;
they shall plant vineyards and eat their fruit.
They shall not build and another inhabit;
they shall not plant and another eat;
for like the days of a tree shall the days of my people be,
and my chosen shall long enjoy the work of their hands.
They shall not labor in vain,
or bear children for calamity;
for they shall be the offspring of the blessed of the LORD,
and their children with them.
Before they call I will answer,
while they are yet speaking I will hear.
The wolf and the lamb shall feed together,
the lion shall eat straw like the ox;
and dust shall be the serpent's food.
They shall not hurt or destroy
in all my holy mountain, says the LORD.

Isaiah 65:17–25

Psalms

The LORD is my shepherd, I shall not want;
he makes me lie down in green pastures.
He leads me beside still waters,
he restores my soul.

He leads me in paths of righteousness
    for his name's sake.

Even though I walk through the valley of the shadow of death,
    I fear no evil;
for thou art with me;
    thy rod and thy staff,
    they comfort me.

Thou preparest a table before me
    in the presence of my enemies;
thou anointest my head with oil,
    my cup overflows.
Surely goodness and mercy shall follow me
    all the days of my life;
and I shall dwell in the house of the LORD
    for ever.   *Psalm 23*

God is our refuge and strength,
    a very present help in trouble.
Therefore we will not fear though the earth should change,
    though the mountains shake in the heart of the sea;
though its waters roar and foam,
    though the mountains tremble with its tumult.

There is a river whose streams make glad the city of God,
    the holy habitation of the Most High.
God is in the midst of her, she shall not be moved;
    God will help her right early.
"Be still, and know that I am God.
    I am exalted among the nations,
    I am exalted in the earth!"
The LORD of hosts is with us;
    the God of Jacob is our refuge.   *Psalm 46:1–5, 10–11*

Lord, thou hast been our dwelling place
    in all generations.
Before the mountains were brought forth,
    or ever thou hadst formed the earth and the world,
    from everlasting to everlasting thou art God.

Thou turnest man back to the dust,
    and sayest, "Turn back, O children of men!"

For a thousand years in thy sight
  are but as yesterday when it is past,
  or as a watch in the night.

Thou dost sweep men away; they are like a dream,
  like grass which is renewed in the morning:
in the morning it flourishes and is renewed;
  in the evening it fades and withers.

For we are consumed by thy anger;
  by thy wrath we are overwhelmed.
Thou hast set our iniquities before thee,
  our secret sins in the light of thy countenance.

For all our days pass away under thy wrath,
  our years come to an end like a sigh.
The years of our life are threescore and ten,
  or even by reason of strength fourscore;
yet their span is but toil and trouble;
  they are soon gone, and we fly away.

So teach us to number our days
  that we may get a heart of wisdom.   *Psalm 90:1–10, 12*

Bless the LORD, O my soul; and all that is within me,
  bless his holy name!
Bless the LORD, O my soul,
  and forget not all his benefits,
who forgives all your iniquity,
  who heals all your diseases,
who redeems your life from the Pit,
  who crowns you with steadfast love and mercy,
who satisfies you with good as long as you live
  so that your youth is renewed like the eagle's.

The LORD works vindication
  and justice for all who are oppressed.
He made known his ways to Moses,
  his acts to the people of Israel.
The LORD is merciful and gracious,
  slow to anger and abounding in steadfast love.
He will not always chide,
  nor will he keep his anger for ever.

He does not deal with us according to our sins,
  nor requite us according to our iniquities.
For as the heavens are high above the earth,
  so great is his steadfast love toward those who fear him;
as far as the east is from the west,
  so far does he remove our transgressions from us.
As a father pities his children
  so the LORD pities those who fear him.
For he knows our frame;
  he remembers that we are dust.

As for man, his days are like grass;
  he flourishes like a flower of the field;
for the wind passes over it, and it is gone,
  and its place knows it no more.
But the steadfast love of the LORD is from everlasting to everlasting
  upon those who fear him,
  and his righteousness to children's children,
to those who keep his covenant
  and remember to do his commandments.

The Lord has established his throne in the heavens,
  and his kingdom rules over all.
Bless the LORD, O you his angels,
  you mighty ones who do his word,
  hearkening to the voice of his word!
Bless the LORD, all his hosts,
  his ministers that do his will!
Bless the LORD, all his works,
  in all places of his dominion.
Bless the LORD, O my soul!   *Psalm 103*

I lift up my eyes to the hills.
  From whence does my help come?
My help comes from the LORD,
  who made heaven and earth.

He will not let your foot be moved,
  he who keeps you will not slumber.
Behold, he who keeps Israel
  will neither slumber nor sleep.

The LORD is your keeper;
　　the LORD is your shade
　　on your right hand.
The sun shall not smite you by day,
　　nor the moon by night.

The LORD will keep you from all evil;
　　he will keep your life.
The LORD will keep
　　your going out and your coming in
　　from this time forth and for evermore.　　　　　*Psalm 121*

Out of the depths I cry to thee, O LORD!
　　Lord, hear my voice!
Let thy ears be attentive
　　to the voice of my supplications!

If thou, O LORD, shouldst mark iniquities,
　　Lord, who could stand?
But there is forgiveness with thee,
　　that thou mayest be feared.

I wait for the LORD, my soul waits,
　　and in his word I hope;
my soul waits for the LORD
　　more than watchmen for the morning,
　　more than watchmen for the morning.

O Israel, hope in the LORD!
　　For with the LORD there is steadfast love,
　　and with him is plenteous redemption.
And he will redeem Israel
　　from all his iniquities.　　　　　*Psalm 130*

O LORD, thou hast searched me and known me!
Thou knowest when I sit down and when I rise up;
　　thou discernest my thoughts from afar.
Thou searchest out my path and my lying down,
　　and art acquainted with all my ways.
Even before a word is on my tongue,
　　lo, O LORD, thou knowest it altogether.
Thou dost beset me behind and before,
　　and layest thy hand upon me.

Such knowledge is too wonderful for me;
  it is high, I cannot attain it.

Whither shall I go from thy Spirit?
  Or whither shall I flee from thy presence?
If I ascend to heaven, thou art there!
  If I make my bed in Sheol, thou art there!
If I take the wings of the morning
  and dwell in the uttermost parts of the sea,
even there thy hand shall lead me,
  and thy right hand shall hold me.
If I say, "Let only darkness cover me,
  and the light about me be night,"
even the darkness is not dark to thee,
  the night is bright as the day;
  for darkness is as light with thee.   *Psalm 139:1–12*

Epistles

For all who are led by the Spirit of God are sons of God. For you did not receive the spirit of slavery to fall back into fear, but you have received the spirit of sonship. When we cry, "Abba! Father!" it is the Spirit himself bearing witness with our spirit that we are children of God, and if children, then heirs, heirs of God and fellow heirs with Christ, provided we suffer with him in order that we may also be glorified with him.

I consider that the sufferings of this present time are not worth comparing with the glory that is to be revealed to us. For the creation waits with eager longing for the revealing of the sons of God; for the creation was subjected to futility, not of its own will but by the will of him who subjected it in hope; because the creation itself will be set free from its bondage to decay and obtain the glorious liberty of the children of God. We know that the whole creation has been groaning in travail together until now; and not only the creation, but we ourselves, who have the first fruits of the Spirit, groan inwardly as we wait for adoption as sons, the redemption of our bodies.

What then shall we say to this? If God is for us, who is against us? He who did not spare his own Son but gave him up for us all, will he not also give us all things with him? Who shall bring any charge against God's elect? It is God who justifies; who is to condemn? Is it

Christ Jesus, who died, yes, who was raised from the dead, who is at the right hand of God, who indeed intercedes for us? Who shall separate us from the love of Christ? Shall tribulation, or distress, or persecution, or famine, or nakedness, or peril, or sword? As it is written,

> "For thy sake we are being killed all the day long;
> we are regarded as sheep to be slaughtered."

No, in all these things we are more than conquerors through him who loved us. For I am sure that neither death, nor life, nor angels, nor principalities, nor things present, nor things to come, nor powers, nor height, nor depth, nor anything else in all creation, will be able to separate us from the love of God in Christ Jesus our Lord.

Romans 8:14–23, 31–39

None of us lives to himself, and none of us dies to himself. If we live, we live to the Lord, and if we die, we die to the Lord; so then, whether we live or whether we die, we are the Lord's. For to this end Christ died and lived again, that he might be Lord both of the dead and of the living.

We shall all stand before the judgment seat of God; for it is written,

> "As I live, says the Lord, every knee shall bow to me,
> and every tongue shall give praise to God."

So each of us shall give account of himself to God.

Romans 14:7–9, 10b–12

Christ has been raised from the dead, the first fruits of those who have fallen asleep. For as by a man came death, by a man has come also the resurrection of the dead. For as in Adam all die, so also in Christ shall all be made alive. But each in his own order: Christ the first fruits, then at his coming those who belong to Christ. Then comes the end, when he delivers the kingdom to God the Father after destroying every rule and every authority and power. For he must reign until he has put all his enemies under his feet. The last enemy to be destroyed is death.

Some one will ask, "How are the dead raised? With what kind of body do they come?" You foolish man! What you sow does not come to life unless it dies. And what you sow is not the body which is to be, but a bare kernel, perhaps of wheat or of some other grain. But

God gives it a body as he has chosen, and to each kind of seed its own body.

So is it with the resurrection of the dead. What is sown is perishable, what is raised is imperishable. It is sown in dishonor, it is raised in glory. It is sown in weakness, it is raised in power. It is sown a physical body, it is raised a spiritual body. If there is a physical body, there is also a spiritual body.

I tell you this, brethren: flesh and blood cannot inherit the kingdom of God, nor does the perishable inherit the imperishable.

For this perishable nature must put on the imperishable, and this mortal nature must put on immortality. When the perishable puts on the imperishable, and the mortal puts on immortality, then shall come to pass the saying that is written:

"Death is swallowed up in victory."
"O death, where is thy victory?
O death, where is thy sting?"

The sting of death is sin, and the power of sin is the law. But thanks be to God, who gives us the victory through our Lord Jesus Christ.

Therefore, my beloved brethren, be steadfast, immovable, always abounding in the work of the Lord, knowing that in the Lord your labor is not in vain.

1 Corinthians 15:20–26, 35–38, 42–44, 50, 53–58

We do not lose heart. Though our outer nature is wasting away, our inner nature is being renewed every day. For this slight momentary affliction is preparing for us an eternal weight of glory beyond all comparison, because we look not to the things that are seen but to the things that are unseen; for the things that are seen are transient, but the things that are unseen are eternal.

For we know that if the earthly tent we live in is destroyed, we have a building from God, a house not made with hands, eternal in the heavens.

2 Corinthians 4:16—5:1

But we would not have you ignorant, brethren, concerning those who are asleep, that you may not grieve as others do who have no hope. For since we believe that Jesus died and rose again, even so, through Jesus, God will bring with him those who have fallen asleep.

For this we declare to you by the word of the Lord, that we who are alive, who are left until the coming of the Lord, shall not precede those who have fallen asleep. For the Lord himself will descend from heaven with a cry of command, with the archangel's call, and with the sound of the trumpet of God. And the dead in Christ will rise first; then we who are alive, who are left, shall be caught up together with them in the clouds to meet the Lord in the air; and so we shall always be with the Lord. Therefore comfort one another with these words.

1 Thessalonians 4:13–18

Then I saw a new heaven and a new earth; for the first heaven and the first earth had passed away, and the sea was no more. And I saw the holy city, new Jerusalem, coming down out of heaven from God, prepared as a bride adorned for her husband; and I heard a loud voice from the throne saying, "Behold, the dwelling of God is with men. He will dwell with them, and they shall be his people, and God himself will be with them; he will wipe away every tear from their eyes, and death shall be no more, neither shall there be mourning nor crying nor pain any more, for the former things have passed away."

And I saw no temple in the city, for its temple is the Lord God the Almighty and the Lamb. And the city has no need of sun or moon to shine upon it, for the glory of God is its light, and its lamp is the Lamb. By its light shall the nations walk; and the kings of the earth shall bring their glory into it, and its gates shall never be shut by day—and there shall be no night there.

There shall no more be anything accursed, but the throne of God and of the Lamb shall be in it, and his servants shall worship him; they shall see his face, and his name shall be on their foreheads. And night shall be no more; they need no light of lamp or sun, for the Lord God will be their light, and they shall reign for ever and ever.

Revelation 21:1–4, 22–25; 22:3–5

Gospels

At that time the disciples came to Jesus, saying, "Who is the greatest in the kingdom of heaven?" And calling to him a child, he put him in the midst of them, and said, "Truly, I say to you, unless you turn and become like children, you will never enter the kingdom of heaven. Whoever humbles himself like this child, he is the greatest in the kingdom of heaven.

"Whoever receives one such child in my name receives me; but whoever causes one of these little ones who believe in me to sin, it would be better for him to have a great millstone fastened round his neck and to be drowned in the depth of the sea.

"See that you do not despise one of these little ones; for I tell you that in heaven their angels always behold the face of my Father who is in heaven."

Matthew 18:1–5, 10

And they were bringing children to him, that he might touch them; and the disciples rebuked them. But when Jesus saw it he was indignant, and said to them, "Let the children come to me, do not hinder them; for to such belongs the kingdom of God. Truly, I say to you, whoever does not receive the kingdom of God like a child shall not enter it." And he took them in his arms and blessed them, laying his hands upon them.

Mark 10:13–16

And when they came to the place which is called The Skull, there they crucified him, and the criminals, one on the right and one on the left.

One of the criminals who were hanged railed at him, saying, "Are you not the Christ? Save yourself and us!" But the other rebuked him, saying, "Do you not fear God, since you are under the same sentence of condemnation? And we indeed justly; for we are receiving the due reward of our deeds; but this man has done nothing wrong." And he said, "Jesus, remember me when you come into your kingdom." And he said to him, "Truly, I say to you, today you will be with me in Paradise."

Luke 23:33, 39–43

Now when Jesus came, he found that Lazarus had already been in the tomb four days. Bethany was near Jerusalem, about two miles off, and many of the Jews had come to Martha and Mary to console them concerning their brother. When Martha heard that Jesus was coming, she went and met him, while Mary sat in the house. Martha said to Jesus, "Lord, if you had been here, my brother would not have died. And even now I know that whatever you ask from God,

God will give you." Jesus said to her, "Your brother will rise again." Martha said to him, "I know that he will rise again in the resurrection at the last day." Jesus said to her, "I am the resurrection and the life; he who believes in me, though he die, yet shall he live, and whoever lives and believes in me shall never die. Do you believe this?" She said to him, "Yes, Lord; I believe that you are the Christ, the Son of God, he who is coming into the world."

John 11:17–27

"Let not your hearts be troubled; believe in God, believe also in me. In my Father's house are many rooms; if it were not so, would I have told you that I go to prepare a place for you? And when I go and prepare a place for you, I will come again and will take you to myself, that where I am you may be also. And you know the way where I am going." Thomas said to him, "Lord, we do not know where you are going; how can we know the way?" Jesus said to him, "I am the way, and the truth, and the life; no one comes to the Father, but by me.

"These things I have spoken to you, while I am still with you. But the Counselor, the Holy Spirit, whom the Father will send in my name, he will teach you all things, and bring to your remembrance all that I have said to you. Peace I leave with you; my peace I give to you; not as the world gives do I give to you. Let not your hearts be troubled, neither let them be afraid."

John 14:1–6, 25–27

COMMENTARY ON THE SERVICES

Christians through the years have expressed what they believe about death, and life after death, through the care they have shown for their dead. Funeral ritual, of course, belongs not only to any particular religious conviction but to the basic heritage of the human community. Margaret Mead expressed a widespread consensus when she remarked, "I know of no people for whom the fact of death is not critical, and who leave no ritual by which to deal with it."[1]

It is not surprising then that early Christian funeral practice should reveal recognizable elements from Greco-Roman culture as well as from its own Judaic roots.[2] From the beginning Christians buried their dead believing in the redemption that their baptism into the death and resurrection of Christ promised (Rom. 6:3–5).

The earliest Christian burial rites retain that glad confidence in the love of God, as seen, for example, in the writings of Cyprian in the mid-third century:

> How often has it been revealed to us that those who have been released from the world by the divine summons ought not to be mourned for, since we know that they are not lost but gone before; while appearing to lose they have really gained ground, as travelers and navigators are wont to do.[3]

However, by the year 1000 the theological ground had significantly shifted, with emphasis on God as a just but terrifying judge. Such a grim feeling, expressed in the well-known medieval hymn the *Dies Irae* ("O Day of Wrath"),[4] characterized many funeral rites, both

Catholic and Protestant, until recent liturgical renewal, which has altered that perception.[5]

Contemporary renewal efforts move away from morose grieving toward sober but glad reaffirmation of the love of God set forth in the gospel. They also try to avoid any implied suggestion that funeral rites are propitiatory or designed to secure or enhance God's favor toward the deceased. It is also evident, as one surveys the funeral liturgies appearing in the last two decades, that they represent a rather remarkable consensus. They all seek to meet the stark fact of death head-on while giving an undaunted witness to resurrection. This commentary intends to illumine the words, sounds, and actions of the service from that perspective.

Ministry to the Dying and the Grieving

In the Presbyterian Church (U.S.A.) "Directory for the Service of God"[6] we find a statement about the intended nature and purpose of a Service of Witness to the Resurrection. All of our ministry at the time of death is shaped by this affirmation:

> The central doctrine of the Christian faith is the resurrection. Christians affirm their common faith in their attitude toward death and in their witness during the approach and experience of death. The reality of death, with all of its attendant sorrow and sense of loss, must be anticipated for us all, and there must be created the kind of health of mind and spirit that allows Christians to live their faith in this critical area of human existence. Christians should seek to make the occasion of death a time in which they reaffirm with joy the hope of the gospel.[7]

This same understanding is reflected in the "Directory for Worship" of the Cumberland Presbyterian Church:

> The belief of Christians in the resurrection from the dead is not a belief which denies the reality of death or suggests that persons have within them some form of immortality. Rather, it is a belief that God's love and power are greater than the power of death, so that though we die and cease to exist, we are given new life, a new existence in God's eternity. All this, Christians affirm because of the resurrection of Jesus Christ from the dead on the first day of the week.[8]

Two services are provided to provide ministry both to the dying and to the bereaved.

Ministry at the Time of Death

The first of these services (pp. 11–17) is for use by the pastor when called to minister to a dying person and to others who are present. Notification about death can be sudden and unexpected, or the culmination of a longer process of illness. In any case there is inescapably a sense of abruptness and finality. The setting for the service can be a home or hospital, or in any of a myriad possible places.

The minister should be sensitive to the most appropriate means to provide ministry, and use the material in the most appropriate manner. In one situation, the prayers may be read from the book. In other circumstances it may be more appropriate to have memorized the material, or to express the themes of the prayers in one's own words.

Human touch can convey comfort and a bond of unity with the dying and those present. While offering the prayers, the minister may hold the hand of the dying person, or place a hand on the dying person's head or shoulder. In providing ministry to the dying, the minister should assume that the dying person is able to hear the prayers, even when vital life signs are failing.

The prayers and Scripture in the "Renewal of Baptism for the Sick and the Dying" in *Holy Baptism and Services for the Renewal of Baptism* (Supplemental Liturgical Resource 2), pp. 92–93, can be particularly helpful for providing the comfort of the scriptural laying on of hands and anointing with oil (James 5:13–16; Mark 16:18b).

If death has already occurred before the minister arrives, the order in this resource may begin with the commendation on page 14, follow with prayers for the bereaved, and conclude with the blessing.

Comforting the Bereaved

In some communities it is customary to gather on the evening before a funeral at the home or the funeral establishment, to pray for those who mourn and to offer assistance to the bereaved. A brief service of prayer is conducted by the pastor or member of the congregation. The order "Comforting the Bereaved" (pp. 18–21) is provided for this purpose. As indicated, prayers, psalms, and lessons contained in the funeral rite are appropriate for this service and may be substituted for those in this order.

Arrangements

The Presbyterian Church (U.S.A.) *Directory* points out:

Christians recognize with all persons the inevitability of death. Because it is difficult under emotional stress to plan or act wisely, the Christian family should make calm appraisal of intents and desires concerning appropriate funeral arrangements before death is imminent.[9]

An increasing number of congregations make provision for putting such "intents and desires" into writing and filing them in the church office where they would be readily available at the time of death. The preparation of such a written statement can benefit from pastoral assistance and the use of a carefully prepared form. The form can deal with preferences about burial, cremation, or donation for medical purposes. Particular wishes about music and selections from Scripture can be made clear, and instructions about a viewing can be given. Information about choice of funeral director, place of burial (or committal in a columbarium), the name of the family lawyer, the location of a will or other papers, or any other details can be set down in advance. Such thoughtful preparation can considerably ease the trauma of death for family and friends.

The Funeral: A Witness to the Resurrection

The Christian funeral service is understood as a service of worship and should be approached as such. Thought should be given to the designing of the service, and it is expected that those present will participate in corporate worship. The singing of hymns, reading of Scripture, preaching of the gospel, confession of sin, affirmation of faith, the celebration of the Lord's Supper are all appropriate to the Christian funeral service.[10]

The service of witness to the resurrection ordinarily should be held in the building set apart for the corporate worship of God. The minister and others who may be properly invited to participate shall be in sole charge of the service.[11]

The service for a believing Christian, as the rubric suggests, should be held in the church, except for compelling reasons (such as lack of adequate space in the church for an expected overflow congregation). In ambiance, architecture, and association the church ties together the major events of the life of faith: Baptism, public profession of faith, Eucharist, marriage, and hope of the resurrection. What better place is there for a funeral? There is less likelihood of introducing alien symbolism if all of these services are held in the church and at its direction.

The Pall and the Procession

The Presbyterian Church (U.S.A.) *Directory* continues:

Because the proper object of the service is the worship of God and the consolation of the living, it follows that the body of the deceased is not necessary to the service. The casket, if it be present during the service, shall be closed at all times and should be covered with a white pall in order that the attention of those assembled may be directed to the Author and Finisher of their salvation.[12]

It should be noted that if the family desires that a viewing be made possible, it should be arranged at some other place and time prior to the service. When the coffin is brought to the church, the pall should be placed over it before it is brought into the sanctuary. The use of a pall avoids calling attention to the relative costliness of the coffin and any invidious comparisons with other funerals. A well designed pall can employ the symbolism of color, fabric, and design that are clearly Christian and the same for all persons, no matter what their state in life (James 2:1–9). In color, the white pall reminds us of our faith in resurrection, and it is furthermore symbolic of our having put on the robe of Christ's righteousness in Baptism.[13]

Two alternate liturgical texts are provided for use in placing the pall on the coffin (pp. 23–24). Each text recalls the centrality of Baptism in the life of a Christian. Galatians 3:27 reminds us that in Baptism we put on the robe of Christ's righteousness. Romans 6:3–5 reminds us that in Baptism we are buried with Christ in his death and raised with him in his resurrection. In the funeral of a Christian, it is particularly appropriate to recall one's baptism. For the faithful Christian, death marks the completion of Baptism, when viewed from the perspective of resurrection.

The words from Galatians or from Romans may be said or sung as the pall is placed upon the coffin at the time the body is received at the entrance of the church. There is special significance in proclaiming these words recalling the beginning of the Christian life in Baptism as the body of one who has faithfully served Christ throughout life enters the church for the last time.

If the pall is placed over the coffin immediately before the procession, the words are sung or said so that the congregation can hear them. The words are not then used in the procession.

Because of the importance of the baptismal focus, Romans 6:3–5 should be used at the funeral of every baptized person. Therefore, if the Romans 6 passage is said before the people assemble, or otherwise not heard by the congregation, it should be included in the sentences of Scripture at the beginning of the service.

By long tradition the most liturgically effective way of bringing the body of the deceased into the place of worship is in procession, after the congregation has assembled and been seated. The usual order: minister(s), lay participants, pallbearers with the coffin (foot first), and the family (if not previously seated). Where the customary liturgical practice of a particular church includes the use of a processional cross and paschal candle, their use in the funeral service would be natural and appropriate. In this case the processional cross leads the procession, followed by the paschal candle. They precede the minister(s) in the procession. As the procession moves forward, a psalm (e.g., 23, 90, 118, 130) or hymn may be sung by the congregation.[14] Or the minister may say the scriptural verses, or sing them using a simple tone.

Placement of the Coffin

The closed coffin should be placed (if architecturally possible) in a position perpendicular to the communion table, rather than crosswise (as if on view).

If a processional cross and paschal candle are part of the procession, the paschal candle is placed in its stand at the head of the coffin, and the cross in its usual place. If the body has been cremated, the urn, if present, should be in place on an appropriate stand in full view of the congregation as the people assemble.

Scripture Sentences

The use of familiar words of Scripture (pp. 24–26) at the beginning of the service helps all present to feel at ease and to participate more effectively. Participation in worship by all the people is one of the distinguishing marks of our tradition. Worship folders may be needed, containing the people's portion of the liturgy, to enable the involvement of the congregation. Special caution must be exercised to avoid the use of non-scriptural texts that compromise or contradict our accepted beliefs.

Music of the Funeral

It is especially important that all music be as carefully chosen as are the Scripture selections, so that everything may be done with dignity, simplicity, and consistency.

Trust and hope in the resurrection, which is proclaimed in the spoken parts of the liturgy, can be reinforced by the church's music. In singing psalms and hymns, Christians express the victory of Christ that is central to the faith, and are renewed and rooted more firmly in the faith. Music for the funeral therefore needs to express the church's faith clearly and to center our attention on those spiritual realities which death cannot destroy.

If a hymn begins the service, either in procession (p. 24) or following the Scripture sentences (p. 26), it should be one of adoration and praise of God and may reflect the liturgical season. A hymn suited to the liturgical season can assist the congregation to see this service in relation to other services of worship of God.

Most of the singing in the service should be done by all those gathered. There is no better way to express the unity of the family of God, and to express the joy and comfort that is integral to the gospel, than for a congregation to sing psalms, hymns, spirituals, and responses together.

In churches where choirs regularly sing in worship on Sunday, it seems appropriate that the choir may also sing for this service as well. When there is a choir, members should assemble quietly and in an orderly way before the service begins. Ordinarily, at a funeral, the choir should not participate in the processions.

All the music of the service should serve the liturgy and have an integral relationship to it. It should never dominate, but always contribute to the spirit and flow of the liturgical action.

Lists of music appropriate for the funeral are included on pp. 87–93.

Prayers

The prayers given here may be used as printed or as guides or models for the preparation of prayers that reflect sensitivity to the particular circumstances. Those who lead the service may wish to augment the selection with prayers of their own choosing or composition. Such individually composed prayers should be simple and direct, giving voice to enduring faith rather than wordy sentimentality. In any case, the prayers should be in language and form that are natural for those praying them.

A prayer of confession may be said by the people followed by a declaration of pardon given by the minister. The prayer of confession that is provided (pp. 28–29) is intentionally simple and universal, avoiding subjectivity.

The rubric following the declaration of pardon suggests that it is appropriate to "sing a thankful response to the mercy of God." Psalm 130 is particularly appropriate and may be sung after the opening prayers, whether or not there is a prayer of confession. The metrical version of Psalm 130 should be familiar to most congregations from use through many years.[15] Other psalms may be used as appropriate to particular situations.[16] *The Service for the Lord's Day* (Supplemental Liturgical Resource 1) also provides texts which may be used.[17]

Since the primary purpose of the service is to thank God for the life of the deceased and for all that it can teach us about the will and purposes of God, caution must always be exercised in our prayers to avoid any impression that we are instructing the Lord about the eternal destiny of the one who has died. In our tradition the memory of abuses connected with prayers for the dead led the Westminster divines to forbid them: "Prayer is to be made for things lawful, and for all sorts of men living, or that shall live hereafter, but not for the dead."[18] The Swiss reformers some eighty years earlier had stated:

> We do not approve of those who are overly and absurdly attentive to the deceased, who, like the heathen, bewail their dead . . . and mumble certain prayers for pay, in order by such ceremonies to deliver their loved ones from the torments in which they are immersed by death, and then think they are able to liberate them by such incantations.[19]

It should be remembered, however, that in the early centuries, before the Apocryphal and so-called Deuterocanonical books were separated from the rest of the canon, prayers for the dead were without apology included in Christian funeral liturgies. Passages such as 2 Maccabees 12:42–45; 15:11–16; and 2 Esdras 2:34–35 were cited for both the warrant and the language for such prayers. Their use in churches accepting the larger canon of Scripture is unbroken since ancient times and is now showing a modest revival.[20] To pray such prayers does not imply belief in purgatory, nor should they be seen as giving the Lord of life instruction about matters that are clearly and solely within the divine prerogative. Affection and concern for anyone dear to us, for whom we have prayed through the years, may lead us quite naturally to continue to do so after this person's death. At least there is no scriptural prohibition against doing so.

Scripture Readings and Sermon

The leader of the service should choose lessons that are appropriate to the life of the person who has died, using selections from both the Old and the New Testament, concluding ordinarily with a passage from the Gospels (pp. 30, 57–74). Laypersons who sustained a significant relationship to the deceased may appropriately be invited to share in this part of the service, although care must be exercised to ensure adequate ability in public reading. The lessons chosen should be acceptable to the one who will preach the sermon, with the further proviso that the preacher be the one to read the lesson immediately preceding the sermon.

The sermon (p. 31) ought always to be a clear proclamation of the gospel but may quite appropriately include grateful reference to the life of the deceased. If desired, several brief tributes may be heard.

Creed

It is particularly appropriate that the Apostles' Creed (p. 31) be said. The Apostles' Creed originated as a baptismal confession of the faith, and it continues to be said when persons are baptized. As such its use in the funeral testifies to the faith into which we are baptized, and by which we live until our baptism is made complete in death when seen from the perspective of resurrection. A musical setting of the Apostles' Creed is included in *The Worshipbook* (no. 259).

The "You are God," or *Te Deum*, is especially appropriate as an affirmation of faith for use in this service and is provided as an alternate liturgical text (p. 52). It proclaims Christ's redemptive work—"You overcame the sting of death, and opened the kingdom of heaven to all believers"—and ends with the petition "Bring us with your saints to glory everlasting."[21]

Some of the affirmations of faith found in *The Service for the Lord's Day* (Supplemental Liturgical Resource 1) are included in the resource (pp. 52–54) as alternate affirmations, because they also commend themselves for use in the funeral.

The Lord's Supper

The celebration of the Sacrament (pp. 34, 37–42) provides a rich and profound opportunity for consolation and strength, with the communion of the saints a visible reality. Decision about celebrating the Lord's Supper, however, should be made only after consultation with the family and authorization by the session of the church. Special care should be exercised to involve elders known to the family, and to plan the details of the service so as to avoid confusion or unnecessary delays. Elders serving the bread and the cup may also be the pallbearers, if desired. The rubrics are simple and direct and ought to be carefully followed. The number and length of the prayers that follow the creed and hymn (p. 31) should be decided with reference to whether the Lord's Supper will be celebrated. If the Supper is not included, the service should proceed directly to the commendation.

Commendation, Blessing, and Procession

Since many present for the service ordinarily do not go to the graveside or columbarium for the committal, a commendation (p. 34) at the close can meet a real need.

The procession then forms as the rubric directs (p. 36), with the presiding minister preceding the body (or ashes). Ashes may be carried by a pallbearer.

The Committal Service

As the rubric states (p. 43), the committal service may take place before the general service at the church is held. This enables family and friends, at the conclusion of the general service, to go directly to a reception which may be held elsewhere in the church building. It is ordinarily at such a reception, when everything else has been tended to and all public services have been completed, that the family can take its first steps toward recovery.

The committal service, whether held before or after the general service, ought to be simple and brief. When the body has been cremated, the ashes in their appropriate container should be placed in the columbarium niche (or other final resting place) in full view of those present.

If the committal is separated from the general service by a significant lapse of time or distance, Scripture lessons and very brief comments may be helpful. The service should close with a blessing. If the entire service is held at the place of committal, prayers like those on pages 26–29 may be used as appropriate.

NOTES

1. "Ritual in Social Crises," in *Roots of Ritual*, ed. James Shaughnessy (Wm. B. Eerdmans Publishing Co., 1973), pp. 89–90.

2. An excellent summary is provided by Richard Rutherford, *The Death of a Christian: The Rite of Funerals* (Pueblo Publishing Co., 1980), pp. 3–36.

3. As quoted by A. S. Duncan-Jones in "The Burial of the Dead" in *Liturgy and Worship* by W. K. Lowther Clarke and Charles Harris (London: S.P.C.K., 1932), p. 618.

4. For the text of this sequence (hymn), in which confidence founded on faith in the resurrection had given way to fear approaching despair, see Rutherford, *The Death of a Christian*, pp. 29, 62.

5. A good bird's-eye view of recent liturgical texts is found on pages 177–178 of *The Service for the Lord's Day* (Supplemental Liturgical Resource 1), prepared by the Joint Office of Worship (Westminster Press, 1984).

6. "Directory for the Service of God," in *The Constitution of the Presbyterian Church (U.S.A.), Part II, Book of Order*, published by the Office of the General Assembly, Presbyterian Church (U.S.A.), Atlanta and New York. Citations in this Commentary are from the edition of 1985–1986.

7. Ibid., "Directory for the Service of God," S-5.0500, first paragraph. Hereafter referred to as "the Presbyterian Church (U.S.A.) *Directory*."

8. "Directory for Worship," in *Confession of Faith and Government of the Cumberland Presbyterian Church, Second Cumberland Presbyterian Church*, published by the Office of the General Assembly, Cumberland Presbyterian Church, 1983, p. 108. Hereafter referred to as "the Cumberland Presbyterian Church *Directory*."

9. The Presbyterian Church (U.S.A.) *Directory*, S-5.0500, third paragraph.

10. The Cumberland Presbyterian Church *Directory*, p. 109.

11. The Presbyterian Church (U.S.A.) *Directory*, S-5.0500, fifth paragraph.

12. Ibid., S-5.0500, sixth paragraph.

13. A number of contemporary baptismal rites include the robing of the newly baptized in a white robe. This custom dates from ancient times and symbolizes the meaning of Baptism expressed in Galatians 3:27: "For as many of you as were baptized into Christ have put on Christ." Where a white robe is customarily given at baptism, the

white pall placed on the coffin of a faithful Christian is a strong reminder of the baptismal robe.

14. Appropriate hymns and suggested musical settings for the psalms are listed on pp. 87–93.

15. The most familiar metrical version of Psalm 130 is "Lord, from the Depths to Thee I Cried" and may be found in hymnals such as: *The Hymnal* (no. 240), *The Hymnbook* (no. 277), and *The Worshipbook* (no. 459). For other musical settings, see p. 90.

16. For musical settings of appropriate psalms, see pp. 89–91.

17. *The Service for the Lord's Day*, liturgical texts 92–97.

18. Westminster Confession, 6.115. For this and the following reference, see *The Constitution of the Presbyterian Church (U.S.A.), Part I, Book of Confessions*, 1983.

19. Second Helvetic Confession, 5.236.

20. See *Book of Common Prayer 1977*, pp. 486 and 502; and Marion J. Hatchett, *Commentary on the American Prayer Book* (Seabury Press, 1981), p. 494. See also *Lutheran Book of Worship*, Ministers Desk Edition (Augsburg Publishing House, and Board of Publication, Lutheran Church in America, 1978), p. 331, item 25; and Philip H. Pfatteicher and Carlos R. Messerli, *Manual on the Liturgy* (Augsburg Publishing House, 1979), p. 363.

21. Musical settings are available in *The Hymnal* (Ancient Hymns and Canticles, no. 49, end with verse 21), and *The Hymnbook* (pp. 589, 590, and 591, end with verse 12). A metrical version is found in *The Worshipbook* (no. 420, "Holy God, We Praise Your Name").

MUSIC FOR THE FUNERAL

Following is a list of music appropriate for the funeral service. A more extensive list of music appropriate for the funeral is available from the Office of Worship of the Presbyterian Church (U.S.A.), 1044 Alta Vista Rd., Louisville, KY 40205.

Hymns

HL	*The Hymnal*
HB	*The Hymnbook*
WB	*The Worshipbook*
*	Opening hymn

	HL	HB	WB
Advent			
Christ, Whose Glory Fills the Skies	26	47	332
*Come, Thou Almighty King	52	244	343
Come, Thou Long-expected Jesus	113	151	342
*Come, You Thankful People, Come	460	525	346
*O Come, O Come, Emmanuel	108	147	489
Christmas			
*All My Heart This Night Rejoices	125	172	—
*All My Heart Today Rejoices	—	—	287
*Good Christian Men, Rejoice	130	165	406
*Hark! the Herald Angels Sing	117	163	411
Once in Royal David's City	454	462	539

	HL	HB	WB
Epiphany			
Christ, Whose Glory Fills the Skies	26	47	332
O Morning Star, How Fair and Bright	321	415	521
Once in Royal David's City	454	462	539
Lent			
*Hosanna, Loud Hosanna (Passion-Palm Sunday)	147	185	424
O Love, How Deep, How Broad	139	—	518
O Love That Wilt Not Let Me Go	307	400	519
Easter			
*Jesus Christ Is Risen Today	163	204	440
*O Sons and Daughters, Let Us Sing!	167	206	527
*The Strife Is O'er, the Battle Done	164	203	597
Ascension			
*Crown Him with Many Crowns	190	213	349
*O for a Thousand Tongues to Sing	199	141	493
The Head That Once Was Crowned with Thorns	—	211	589
Pentecost			
Christ Is Made the Sure Foundation	336	433	325
*Holy, Holy, Holy! (Trinity)	57	11	421
How Firm a Foundation	283	369	425
General			
A Mighty Fortress Is Our God	266	91	274,
	—	—	276
For All the Saints	429	425	369
Give to the Winds Your Fears	294	364	377
God of Our Life	88	108	395
*Holy God, We Praise Your Name	—	—	420
*I Greet Thee, Who My Sure Redeemer Art	—	144	625
O Love That Wilt Not Let Me Go	307	400	519
*Praise, My Soul, the King of Heaven	14	31	551
Praise We Our Maker While We've Breath	—	—	558
*We Come Unto Our Fathers' God	342	16	623
*We Greet You, Sure Redeemer from All Strife	—	144	625

Psalms

Resources cited below, in addition to the hymnals, are:
The Gelineau Gradual (Chicago: G.I.A. Publications, Inc., 1969, 1975, 1977), a collection of responsorial psalms from The Grail/Gelineau Psalter. Order from: G.I.A. Publications, Inc., 7404 S. Mason Ave., Chicago, IL 60638 (Order no. G-2124).

A Psalm Sampler (Philadelphia: The Westminster Press, 1986), developed by the Office of Worship. A collection of 29 settings of psalms and biblical songs in a variety of musical styles. It may be ordered from Materials Distribution Service, 341 Ponce de Leon Ave., N.E., Atlanta, GA 30365, or a Cokesbury Service Center.

Gradual Psalms (Church Hymnal Series VI) (New York: The Church Hymnal Corporation, 1980, 1981, 1982). A three-volume collection of Gregorian psalm tones. Order from The Church Hymnal Corporation, 800 Second Ave., New York, NY 10017.

	HL	HB	WB
Psalm 23			
Metrical version: The Lord's My Shepherd	97	104	592, 593
Gelineau: The Lord Is My Shepherd. *The Gelineau Gradual*, p. 136			
Responsorial: The Lord Is My Shepherd. *A Psalm Sampler*			
Psalm 27			
Metrical version: God Is Our Strong Salvation	92	347	388
Psalm 42			
Metrical version: As Pants the Hart for Cooling Streams	317	322	—
Metrical version: As the Deer in Summer's Heat. *A Psalm Sampler*			
Psalm 46			
Metrical version: God Is Our Refuge and Our Strength	91	381	—
Choral: Contemporary setting, "Psalm 46," from *Three Psalms of Celebration*, by Arthur Wills, published by The Royal School of Church Music			

Organ Repertoire

Bach, J. S.
  All Men Are Mortal *(Orgelbüchlein)*
  Christ Lay in Death's Dark Prison *(Orgelbüchlein)*
  Fugue in E-flat Major (St. Anne)
  Sheep May Safely Graze
  When We Are in Deepest Need (Before Thy Throne I Now Appear)
Brahms, Johannes
  Selections from Eleven Chorale Preludes (H. W. Gray)
Buxtehude, Dietrich
  We Pray Now to the Holy Spirit (Nun bitten wir)
Davies, H. Walford
  Solemn Melody
Johnson, David N.
  A Mighty Fortress (Augsburg)
Mendelssohn, Felix
  "Andante tranquillo" from *Sonata III*
  "Finale" from *Sonata VI*
Peeters, Flor
  Elegy (Peters)
Reger, Max
  Benedictus (Marks)
Vaughan Williams, Ralph
  Prelude on "Rhosymedre" (Stainer and Bell)
Walther, Johann G.
  Praise to the Lord, the Almighty (Concordia)
  A Mighty Fortress Is Our God (Concordia)
Wright, Searle
  Prelude on "Brother James' Air" (Psalm 23) (Oxford)

Choral Music

[E]   Easy
[M]   Medium
[D]   Difficult

Unison, Two-Part, and Three-Part

Blest Are They Whose Spirits Long, G. F. Handel; arr. H. Hopson. Two-Part

"Dona nobis pacem" arr. H. Hopson. Three-Part

"In dulci jubilo," D. Buxtehude. SAB, 2 violins, 2 flutes, and continuo (Concordia 98-1501) (Christmas)

I Will Not Leave You Comfortless, Ron Nelson. Unison. *Four Anthems for Young Choirs* (Boosey & Hawkes, No. 5576)

Jesu, Joy of Man's Desiring, J.S. Bach. Two-Part (Belwin, No. 937)

O How Amiable (Pss. 84 and 90, ending with "O God, Our Help in Ages Past"), Ralph Vaughan Williams. Two-Part Mixed (Oxford University Press MA94) [E]

Se Il Signore Mio Pastore (God the Lord, He Is My Shepherd), Benedetto Marcello. SA, TB, or Two-Part Mixed (in *Sing Joyfully*, Vol. 2, Walton Music Corp.)

SATB Anthems

Brother James' Air (Psalm 23), Gordon Jacobs (Oxford)

E'en So, Lord Jesus, Quickly Come, Paul Manz (Concordia 98-1054) (Advent)

I Will Lift Up My Eyes, Leo Sowerby (Boston Music and G. Schirmer) [EM]

I Will Not Leave You Comfortless, William Byrd (Novello)

I Will Not Leave You Comfortless, Titcomb (Carl Fischer)

Lord, Thou Hast Been Our Refuge, Ralph Vaughan Williams (G. Schirmer 9720) [D]

My Shepherd Will Supply My Need, Virgil Thomson (H. W. Gray CMR2046) [E]

O How Amiable, Ralph Vaughan Williams (Oxford 42056) [E]

O Lord, Support Us, Maurice Besly (Novello)

Sheep May Safely Graze, J. S. Bach (Cathedral Press)

"Sine nomine" (For All the Saints), Ralph Vaughan Williams

The Eyes of All Wait Upon Thee, Jean Berger

The Lord Is My Shepherd, Thomas Matthews (H. T. Fitz-
Simons 2137-7) [EM]
The Lord Is My Shepherd, John Rutter (Oxford) [M]
Who Shall Separate Us, Heinrich Schütz (Chantry) [M]

Choral Music from Larger Works
Elijah, Felix Mendelssohn
Cast Thy Burden Upon the Lord. SATB
He Watching Over Israel. SATB
Lift Thine Eyes. SSA
German Requiem, Johannes Brahms
How Lovely Is Thy Dwelling Place. SATB
Messiah, G. F. Handel
Since by Man Came Death. SATB

Vocal Solos

I Will Lift Up Mine Eyes, Leo Sowerby. Low voice (H. W. Gray)
Jesus, Redeemer, Our Loving Savior, Anton Bruckner (Peters)
Jesus, Shepherd, Be Thou Near Me, J. S. Bach (Peters)
Who Shall Separate Us, Daniel Pinkham. Baritone (Peters)

SOURCES OF THE LITURGICAL TEXTS

ASB   *The Alternative Service Book 1980*. Church of England, 1980.
BCO   *The Book of Common Order (1979)*. Church of Scotland, 1979.
BCP   *The Book of Common Prayer*. Episcopal Church, U.S.A., 1977.
BCW   *The Book of Common Worship*. Presbyterian, U.S.A., 1946.
BS   *The Book of Services*. The United Methodist Church, U.S.A.,
        1985.
LBW   *Lutheran Book of Worship*. Lutheran, U.S.A., 1978.
OCC   *Occasional Services*. Lutheran, U.S.A., 1982.
OCF   *Order of Christian Funerals*. International Commission on
        English in the Liturgy (Roman Catholic), 1985.
UCA   *Uniting Church Worship Services: Funeral*. The Uniting Church
        in Australia, 1984.
UCC   *Proposed Services of Memorial and Thanksgiving*, 1982.
        United Church of Christ, U.S.A., 1982.
WBK   *The Worshipbook—Services and Hymns*. Presbyterian, U.S.A.,
        1972.

Abbreviations for Bible translations are:
JB   *The Jerusalem Bible*
NEB   *The New English Bible*
PHI   *The New Testament in Modern English*, J. B. Phillips
RSV   *Revised Standard Version*
TEV   *Today's English Version (Good News Bible)*

All Scripture quotations are from the RSV except as noted. The following quotations are altered: Num. 6:24–26 (pp. 17, 50); Job 19:25 (p.

43); Ps. 16:9 (p. 44); Ps. 16:11 (p. 44); Isa. 66:13 (p. 25); Matt. 11:28 (p. 25); John 6:37 (p. 44); John 11:25–26 (p. 24); Rom. 8:1, 28, 38–39 (pp. 53–54); Rom. 8:35, 37–39 (p. 53); Rom. 14:7–8 (pp. 26, 44); Rom. 15:13 (p. 18); Phil. 4:7 (pp. 36, 50); Heb. 13:20–21 (pp. 35, 51); Rev. 14:13 (pp. 26, 44, 45).

Rom. 6:3–5 (pp. 23–24) is based upon RSV, NEB, and TEV.

2 Cor. 1:3–4 (pp. 18, 26) is based upon RSV, NEB, and JB.

1 Thess. 4:14, 17–18 (p. 26) is based upon RSV, NEB, JB, and PHI.

1 Peter 1:3–4 (p. 25) is from NEB and is altered.

Rom. 8:34 (p. 29); and 2 Cor. 5:17 (p. 29) are from PHI and are altered.

Sources of liturgical texts are acknowledged as follows:

p. 12—"Lord Jesus Christ . . ." BCP, adapted.

p. 12—"Almighty God, by your power . . ." WBK, revised.

p. 13—"_____ , our *brother/sister* in the faith . . ." OCC, altered from the Roman Catholic Rite for the Commendation of the Dying.

p. 13—"God of compassion and love . . ." OCC.

p. 13—"Depart in peace . . ." BCP, adapted.

p. 14—"Into your hands . . ." BCP.

pp. 14, 46—"O Lord, support us . . ." BCW, WBK, altered; attributed to John Henry Newman (1801–1890).

p. 15—"Lord Jesus, we wait . . ." UCA, adapted.

p. 16—"Merciful God, you strengthen . . ." UCA.

p. 16—"Gracious God, in darkness . . ." UCA, altered.

p. 19—"Jesus said, 'Come to me . . .' " BCP, adapted.

p. 20—"Almighty God, source of . . ." LBW.

pp. 21, 49—"Loving God, your beloved . . ." LBW, adapted.

p. 26—"Eternal God, Father of . . ." BCW, altered.

p. 27—"O God, who gave us birth . . ." BS, altered.

p. 27—"Eternal God, we bless you . . ." BS, altered.

p. 28—"Eternal God amid all the changes . . ." BCW, revised; scriptural allusions are: Ps. 39:5; Isa. 40:6–8; Ps. 23:4; and Ps. 39:4, 12.

p. 29—"Who is in a position . . ." WBK, altered.

p. 29—"The mercy of the Lord . . ." BCW (1906, 1932, and 1946), revised.

p. 30—"Eternal God, your love . . ." BCW, revised.

p. 31—"I believe in God . . ." This text for the Apostles' Creed is the agreed ecumenical text prepared by the International Consultation on English Texts.

p. 31—"O God of grace . . ." BCW and WBK, revised.

p. 32—"O God, before whom generations . . ." WBK, revised.

p. 32—"Almighty God, in Jesus Christ . . ." WBK, revised.

p. 33—"For our *brother/sister* _____ ," OCF and BCP, altered.

p. 34—"Loving Father, you are nearest . . ." Based upon prayers in the BCO (1940 and 1979).

p. 34—"You only are immortal . . ." BCP, altered.

p. 35—"Holy God, by your creative power . . ." UCC, altered.

p. 35—"Into your hands, O merciful Savior . . ." BCP, altered.

p. 36—"The peace of God . . ." BCW (1906, 1932, 1946), revised.

p. 36—"May God in endless mercy . . ." ASB, altered.

p. 36—"Lord, now you let . . ." This text for the *Nunc dimittis* is the agreed ecumenical text prepared by the International Consultation on English Texts.

pp. 37–40—The Great Prayer of Thanksgiving. The opening dialogue (p. 37) is an agreed ecumenical text prepared by the international Consultation on English Texts, with one slight alteration. In the last line the Consultation's text reads: "give him thanks." The text in this resource reads: "give our thanks." The "Holy, holy, holy Lord . . ." (p. 38) is an agreed ecumenical text prepared by the International Consultation on English Texts. The acclamation "Dying you destroyed . . ." (p. 39) is from the sacramentary of the Roman Catholic Church (1974).

pp. 40, 46—"Our Father in heaven . . ." is an agreed ecumenical text prepared by the International Consultation on English Texts.

p. 41—"Because there is . . ." Based on NEB text of 1 Cor. 10:16–17.

p. 41—"The Lord Jesus, on the night . . ." Based on the RSV text of 1 Cor. 11:23–26, and Luke 22:19–20.

p. 41—"The gifts of God . . ." BCP. Derives from fourth-century Eastern liturgies: "The holy for the holy" or "Holy things for holy people."

p. 42—"Jesus, Lamb of God . . ." and "Lamb of God, you take . . ." are agreed ecumenical texts prepared by the International Consultation on English Texts.

p. 42—"Almighty God, we thank you . . ." BCP.

p. 43—"The Sun of Righteousness . . ." BCP.

p. 43—"The Lord will guide our feet . . ." BCP.

p. 44—"Christ is risen from the dead . . ." BCP, altered. Based upon an antiphon sung in the Eastern Byzantine Easter liturgy. At a burial during the Easter season, it is sung as the body is carried to the grave.

p. 46—"O God, you have designed . . ." WBK, altered.

p. 47—"God of all mercies and giver of all comfort . . ." UCA, altered.

p. 47—"Gracious Father, in darkness and in light . . ." UCA.

p. 47—"Almighty God, Father of . . ." WBK.

p. 48—"God of all consolation . . ." UCA, altered.

p. 48—"O God, whose mercies . . ." UCA, altered.

p. 49—"God, whose days . . ." Based upon a prayer in the committal of the Roman Catholic funeral rite.

p. 49—"Rest eternal grant . . ." BCP, LBW, OCF. From 2 Esdras 2:34–35. This antiphon, common to funeral liturgies of the West, dates from at least the ninth century. "Requiem," the term for a Eucharist for the departed, derives from the first word of the Latin text of this antiphon.

p. 49—"Loving God, give us faith . . ." WBK, altered.

p. 52—"You are God . . ." The "You are God . . ." (Te Deum), is believed to date from at least the fourth century, although the oldest manuscript dates from the seventh century. A medieval legend states that Ambrose and Augustine composed it extemporaneously at Augustine's baptism. It is more likely that it is the work of Nicetas, bishop of Remesiana in Dacia (c. 392–414). Similar to a eucharistic prayer, it may have been written for that purpose.

p. 54—"This is the good news . . ." WBK, altered. It is formed of a composite of Scriptures: 1 Cor. 15:1–6; Mark 16:9 (16:1–9); Matt. 16:16; Rev. 22:13; and John 20:28.

p. 54—"Almighty God, you call . . ." LBW, altered.

p. 56—"O God, we thank you . . ." BCW, revised.

BIBLIOGRAPHICAL ESSAY

Concern for the pastoral care of the dying and the bereaved has been marked in the last generation and among other things has produced devotional and pastoral material. Elisabeth Kübler-Ross has been widely influential among ministers through *On Death and Dying* (Macmillan Co., 1969) and *Questions and Answers on Death and Dying* (Macmillan Publishing Co., 1975). Henri Nouwen has offered some fruits of his ministry to his own parents at his mother's dying (*In Memoriam*, 1970; *Letter of Consolation*, 1982). Granger Westberg contributed *Good Grief* (Fortress Press, 1962). Two of the essays in G. Cope (ed.), *Dying, Death and Disposal* (London: S.P.C.K., 1970) have this character. This is also the approach of Paul Irion in *The Funeral and the Mourners* (Abingdon Press, 1954) and *The Funeral: Vestige or Value?* (Abingdon Press, 1966).

With regard to burial practices and rites there seems to be no comprehensive history of the Christian funeral. Geoffrey Powell's *Liturgy of Christian Burial: An Introductory Survey of the Historical Development of Christian Burial Rites* (London: S.P.C.K., 1977) is a helpful beginning, but is largely confined to Anglicanism for the Reformation and modern periods. This lack is particularly repaired by the article on "Burial" in J. G. Davies's *Dictionary of Liturgy and Worship* (Macmillan Co., 1972). (Rev. ed. published by Westminster Press as *The New Westminster Dictionary of Liturgy and Worship*, 1986.)

There are also general histories of worship which include significant treatment of the Reformed tradition. See, for example, W. Maxwell's *Outline of the History of Worship* (London, 1936), or Horton Davies's five volumes, published by Princeton University Press: *Worship and Theology in England: From Cranmer to Hooker, 1534–1603* (1970); *From Andrewes to Baxter and Fox, 1603–1690* (1975); *From Watts and Wesley to Maurice* (1961); *From Newman to Martineau* (1962); and *The Ecumenical Century, 1900–1965* (1965); and his *Worship of the English Puritans* (Westminster Press, 1948).

Howard Hageman, *Pulpit and Table* (John Knox Press, 1962), and James Nichols, *Corporate Worship in the Reformed Tradition* (Westminster Press, 1968), attempt brief interpretations of the Reformed tradition but lack consideration of funerals. There are also histories of Reformed worship in specific countries, as W. Maxwell, *A History of Worship in the Church of Scotland* (London: Oxford University Press, 1955); J. D. Benoit, *Initiations à la liturgie de l'Eglise réformé de France* (Paris, 1956); Eugene Bersier, *Liturgie à l'usage des Eglises réformées* (Paris, 1875); Emile Doumergue, *Essai sur l'histoire du culte réformé . . . au xvie et au xixe siècle* (Paris, 1890); and J. Melton, *Presbyterian Worship in America* (John Knox Press, 1967). J. H. O. Ebrard, *Reformiertes Kirchenbuch* (Zurich, 1847), edits for modern use a series of five burial prayers from four different Reformed liturgies: Zurich, 1612; the *Book of Common Prayer;* St. Gallen, 1738; Schaffhausen, 1672. These studies of regional or national churches often contain material on burial thought and practices.

The several Reformed churches may be considered in a spectrum of liturgical practice. In general, the Continental churches—Swiss, Dutch, German, Hungarian—and the Church of England adopted fuller forms than the churches in England, Scotland, and the American colonies that were significantly influenced by the Puritan movement. Of all these liturgies, the Anglican *Book of Common Prayer* has exhibited the greatest literary distinction and has had the widest influence, despite the somewhat ambiguous character of its relation to the Reformed tradition. Beginning with the first prayer book of 1549, followed by the revision of 1552, and the Elizabethan book of 1559, the *Book of Common Prayer* has undergone several revisions (see the *New History of the Book of Common Prayer* by Proctor and W. H. Frere, Macmillan, 1901, and M. J. Hatchett's *Commentary on the American Prayer Book,* Seabury Press, 1981, especially the section on "Burial of the Dead").

Comparable in general character, while inferior in style, is the Palatinate Liturgy of 1563, the most important of the German Reformed orders. The Palatinate Liturgy was largely built on the Dutch, but added considerable material on visitation of the sick and burial of the dead which had not been included in the Dutch service book. The tolling of bells during the solemn walk to the grave, choristers when available singing psalms, Scripture reading (1 Thess. 4:14 and John 11:1–47), and themes for preaching were provided.

At the other end of the liturgical spectrum were the Puritans in England, Scotland, and the American colonies. They feared the abuses most of all of the cult of saints, and prayers to and for the dead, which attended medieval Roman Catholic funerals. They generally omitted spoken or sung prayers, readings, and sometimes even sermons. What was to become the Puritan attitude can be illustrated from the first Scottish service book, composed by refugees from Queen Mary's persecution and known inaccurately as *John Knox' Genevan Service Book* (ed. W. Maxwell, Edinburgh and London, 1931). The burial order of this book provided that the congregation should reverently attend the body to the grave and witness the burial in silence, then to the church, if not too far, where the minister would deliver "some comfortable exhortation to the people, touchyng death and resurrection." Ministers were thus left to their own resources for prayer and sermon, and indeed their presence was not considered essential to the service. Burial, like marriage, was understood as civil rather than ecclesiastical action.

The "John Knox" book was replaced in Scotland nearly a century later by the *Westminster Directory* (ed. T. Leishman, Edinburgh, 1901). The Directory was to become the classical liturgical manual of Puritans on both sides of the Atlantic until well into the nineteenth century. Prayers, spoken or sung, and scripture readings were generally omitted on the way to or at the grave. Such was the prevalent practice among Presbyterians, Congregationalists, and to a considerable extent, also Baptists. At the "anti-liturgical" end of the Reformed spectrum, New England Puritanism showed itself less strict than that of old England. (See David E. Stannard, *The Puritan Way of Death*, Oxford University Press, 1977, and Gordon E. Geddes, *Welcome Joy: Death in Puritan New England*, UMI Research Press, 1981.)

The middle generation of the nineteenth century saw a turning of the tide in the Reformed churches with regard to worship. A steady or increasing leakage of ministers and laymen from the Puritan denominations to the Episcopal fold demonstrated the growing attractiveness of the *Book of Common Prayer*. A variety of publications argued that the heirs of the Puritans should recover their liturgical heritage. Ebrard's *Reformiertes Kirchenbuch* was a selection of largely sixteenth-, seventeenth-, and eighteenth-century prayers, arranged for modern use. C. W. Baird's *Eutaxia, or the Presbyterian Liturgies* (New York, 1855), urged the use of such forms as the Lord's Prayer and the Apostles' Creed and demonstrated how these had been used in the Reformation churches. Charles Shields published in 1864 the *Presbyterian Book of Common Prayer*, which attempted to show what the result would have been if the revision committee of 1661 had adopted the recommendations of the Puritan minority of the delegation. The argument is indicated by a formidable title: *The Book of Common Prayer . . . as amended by the Presbyterian Divines in the Royal Commission of 1661 and in agreement with the Directory for Public Worship of the Presbyterian Church . . . with a supplementary treatise* (New York, 1864). After some years, Professor Shields gave up the fight and entered the Anglican communion. Eugene Bersier, the most famous French Protestant preacher of his day, made a study of worship, both that of the French Reformed Church historically, and that of other churches, such as the Anglican. His own church in Paris demonstrated his program in practice (*Liturgie*, 1876).

Up to the middle of the nineteenth century most of the fresh liturgical texts in Reformed churches represented the achievement of individuals. Two exceptions may be noted: "The Liturgy" of the Catholic Apostolic Church was, to be sure, apparently the work of one reformer, John Cardale, but it was adopted and propagated officially by a *church*, however small. Similarly, the German Reformed Church in the United States accepted, after extended controversy, a *Provisional Liturgy* (1857) and then an *Order of Worship* (1867) which was likewise an official, though not mandated, liturgical platform of a denomination. The influence of both the *Book of Common Prayer* and the Catholic Apostolic Liturgy was unmistakable, but the whole was put together with notable skill. In Scotland a "Church Service Society" was organized for liturgical research and thought. The first of their publications, *Euchologion* (1867) did not vary much from the *Book of Common Prayer* in its burial service and was also indebted to the American German Reformed, and the Catholic Apostolic liturgy.

At the end of the nineteenth century two Presbyterian churches, the English (1890) and the American (1906) followed the precedent of the Catholic

Apostolic Church and the German Reformed by authorizing a service book that was, on the one hand, for voluntary use and, on the other, officially sanctioned. This pattern was to become general in the twentieth century, with the French, Dutch, Scottish, and Swiss as well as churches in formerly colonial areas, as Canada and Australia. Along with this new quasi-official status for service books, the succession of contributions by individuals continued and increased. Half of the prayers in Herrick Johnsen's *Forms for Special Occasions* (1889) were for burials.

About the time of World War II a notable group of official service books appeared. The Scottish *Book of Common Order* (1940) had significant influence on the American Presbyterian *Book of Common Worship* (1946). About the same time came the *Liturgie* of the canton Vaud, and a little later (1955) the *Liturgie* of the Reformed Church of France. This generation of texts often bore the marks of the ecumenical movement, the biblical and theological revival, and patristic studies. It is harder to assess what effect they had on the congregations using them.

In the second half of the twentieth century a significant literature on death, burial, and related matters has appeared, expressing an anthropological or sociological perspective rather than a theological one. In considerable measure these writings represent a critical reaction to widespread sentimentality and commercialization. Jessica Mitford's *The American Way of Death* (Simon & Schuster, 1963) is one of the more famous. Over half of the dead in Great Britain are now cremated rather than buried. A school of sociological historians in France has demonstrated how views and practices on death and burial can illuminate many dimensions of a culture that would not seem at first glance to be related:

Russell Aldwinckler, *Death in the Secular City* (Wm. B. Eerdmans, 1972)
Philippe Ariès, *Western Attitudes Toward Death* (Johns Hopkins University Press, 1974)
———, *The Hour of Our Death* (Alfred A. Knopf, 1981)
Ernest Becker, *The Denial of Death* (Free Press, 1973)
Richard R. Dumont and Dennis Foss, *The American View of Death: Acceptance or Denial?* Schenkman Publishing Co., 1972)
Geoffrey Gorer, *Death, Grief and Mourning in Contemporary Britain* (Doubleday & Co., 1965)
Arien Mack (ed.), *Death in American Experience* (Schocken Books, 1972)
John McManners, *Death and the Enlightenment* (Oxford University Press, 1981)

Theology deals with some of the same phenomena as the sociologists but speaks specifically for the Christian community on such topics as death, judgment, resurrection.

Karl Barth, *Church Dogmatics*, III/2 (Edinburgh: T. & T. Clark, 1960)
Hendrikus Berkhof, *A Well-Founded Hope* (John Knox Press, 1969)
Ladislaus Boros, *The Mystery of Death* (Herder & Herder, 1965)
Louis Evely, *In the Face of Death* (Seabury Press, 1979)
Monika Hellwig, *What Are They Saying About Death and Christian Hope?* (Paulist Press, 1978)

Eberhard Jüngel, *Death: The Riddle and the Mystery* (Westminster Press, 1974)

John Macquarrie, *Studies in Christian Existentialism* (Westminster Press, 1966)

Jürgen Moltmann, *The Crucified God* (Harper & Row, 1974)

Johannes Quasten, *Music and Worship in Pagan and Christian Antiquity,* tr. Boniface Ramsey. (National Association of Pastoral Musicians). See esp. ch. 6, "Music and Singing in the Pagan and Christian Cults of the Dead."

Karl Rahner, *On the Theology of Death* (Herder & Herder, 1961)

Edward Schillebeeckx, *The Layman in the Church* (Alba House, 1963)

Krister Stendahl (ed.), *Immortality and Resurrection* (Macmillan Co., 1965)

Helmut Thielicke, *Death and Life* (Fortress Press, 1970)

Daniel P. Walker, *The Decline of Hell* (University of Chicago Press, 1964)

The following service books containing funeral liturgy or, in two cases, commentaries, are arranged by denominations:

Lutheran Book of Worship, Ministers Desk Edition. Inter-Lutheran Commission on Worship. Published by Augsburg Publishing House, Minneapolis, and Board of Publications, Lutheran Church in America, Philadelphia.

Manual on the Liturgy: Lutheran Book of Worship. Philip H. Pfatteicher and Carlos S. Messerli. Augsburg Publishing House, Minneapolis, 1979

The Book of Common Worship. Presbyterian Church in the U.S.A., 1946

The Worshipbook. Westminster Press, Philadelphia, 1970

Confession of Faith. Cumberland Presbyterian Church

The Book of Common Order. Saint Andrew Press, Edinburgh, 1979

Uniting Church Worship Services. Joint Board of Christian Education of Australia and New Zealand. Uniting Church Press, 177 Collins Street, Melbourne 3000, Australia

A Book of Services. The United Reformed Church in England and Wales. Saint Andrew Press, Edinburgh, 1980

The Book of Common Prayer. Episcopal Church. The Church Hymnal Corporation, New York, and Seabury Press, 1977

Commentary on the American Prayer Book. Marion J. Hatchett. Seabury Press, 1981

The Alternative Service Book, 1980. Church of England. S.P.C.K. and Cambridge University Press

The Roman Ritual. Revised by Decree of the Second Vatican Council and published by Authority of Pope Paul VI. The Liturgical Press, Collegeville, MN, 1971

The Book of Services. United Methodist Church, 1985

The Fall 1986 issue of *Reformed Liturgy and Music* will be particularly useful in relation to *The Funeral: A Service of Witness to the Resurrection.* The theme of the issue will be the funeral, and it will include practical articles on planning and leading the funeral. Copies may be secured from the Office of Worship (1044 Alta Vista Rd., Louisville, KY 40205) when it is published.

ACKNOWLEDGMENTS

Material from the following sources is acknowledged and is used by permission. Adaptations are by permission of copyright holders.

Scripture quotations from the *Revised Standard Version of the Bible* are copyrighted 1946, 1952, © 1971, 1973 by the Division of Christian Education of the National Council of the Churches of Christ in the U.S.A.

The Scripture quotations from *The New English Bible* are copyright © The Delegates of the Oxford University Press and The Syndics of the Cambridge University Press 1961, 1970.

The Scripture quotations from *The New Testament in Modern English*, translated by J. B. Phillips, revised edition, are copyright © J. B. Phillips, 1958, 1959, 1966, 1972. Used by permission of Macmillan Publishing Company, Inc.

The Apostles' Creed (p. 31), the preface dialogue (p. 37) "Holy, holy, holy Lord" (p. 38), the Lord's Prayer (pp. 40, 46), "Jesus, Lamb of God" (p. 42), and "Lord, now you let your servant go in peace" (p. 36), are from *Prayers We Have in Common*, copyright © 1970, 1971, and 1975 by International Consultation on English Texts.

The Book of Common Worship, copyright © 1932 and 1946 by The Board of Christian Education of the Presbyterian Church in the United States of America. Used by permission of The Westminster Press.

The Worshipbook—Services, copyright © MCMLXX The Westminster Press. Used by permission of The Westminster Press.